READ:
Seventy Strategies to Support Reading Success

Kimberly Kimbell-Lopez
Carrice Cummins

WILEY

JOHN WILEY & SONS, INC.

VP & EXECUTIVE PUBLISHER	Jay O' Callaghan
ACQUISITIONS EDITOR	Robert Johnston
SENIOR PRODUCTION EDITOR	Nicole Repasky
MARKETING MANAGER	Danielle Torio
SENIOR DESIGNER	Kevin Murphy
PRODUCTION MANAGEMENT SERVICES	Aptara®, Inc.
MEDIA EDITOR	Bridget O'Lavin
EDITORIAL ASSISTANT	Aaron Talwar
COVER PHOTO	© Jani Bryson/iStockphoto

This book was set in StoneSerif by Aptara®, Inc. and printed and bound by Bind-Rite/Robbinsville. The cover was printed by Bind-Rite/Robbinsville.

This book is printed on acid free paper. ∞

Library of Congress Cataloging-in-Publication Data
Kimbell-Lopez, Kimberly.
  READ : seventy strategies to support student success/Kimberly Kimbell-Lopez,
Carrice Cummins.
     p. cm.
  Include index.
  ISBN 978-0-470-52103-8 (pbk. : alk. paper)
  1. Literacy. 2. Reading comprehension. 3. Oral communication.
4. Written Communication. I. Cummins, Carrice, 1955– II. Title.
  LC149.K56 2009
  372.6'044–dc22
                                                        2009016547

Printed in the United States of America

10 9 8 7 6 5 4 3 2 1

Contents

Introduction

Reading is a complex task comprised of numerous skills and processes that interact to make meaning. Skilled readers use a variety of strategies to help them make meaning of text; however, most readers do not develop these skills and processes on their own. Excellent teachers who are knowledgeable about a wide variety of instructional strategies are key to helping students become strategic readers (IRA 2000). Effective teachers provide explicit ongoing instruction that introduces, models, explains, and helps students apply literacy strategies interactively and continuously when they read.

The National Reading Panel (2000) identified five major reading skill areas essential to effective reading instruction: phonemic awareness, phonics, fluency, vocabulary, and comprehension. These elements are indeed crucial to the development of reading; however, limiting the focus of reading instruction to these five areas might preclude emphasis on other important areas of literacy development, such as oral language and writing. Teachers need to use strategies that allow students to be actively engaged in all seven of these literacy processes.

READ: Seventy Strategies to Support Student Success will assist teachers in their endeavor to help students become strategic readers. This edition is a collection of strategies based on the 5 + 2 essential elements of literacy instruction: oral language, phonemic awareness, phonics, fluency, vocabulary, comprehension, and writing. The text is intended to be a teacher-friendly document that teachers can use to provide students with strategies for developing a clearer understanding of these areas of literacy development. The strategies provided represent only a small sample of the numerous strategies and activities that teachers can use in strengthening students' skills in each of the identified areas. We realize that the term *strategies* has taken on many different definitions over time and is often used interchangeably with terms such as *activities* and *methods*. For this reason, some of the strategies included in this book could be referred to as activities, methods, or even approaches.

The book is divided into eight sections representing seven elements of instruction plus a section containing strategies utilized in the development of a reading curriculum framework. Each section contains a brief conceptual overview as well as specific strategies that can be used to facilitate the development of that literacy process. Each strategy follows an R.E.A.D. format:

R—rationale of the strategy
E—explanation of the strategy
A—application of the strategy
D—delivery of the strategy

The rationale of the strategy (R) explains why the strategy is important in developing strategic readers as it applies to that particular literacy element. The strategy explanation (E) more explicitly defines and describes the critical characteristics the strategy encompasses. The application (A) section provides a descriptive narrative of what the strategy might look like in the classroom. Step-by-step procedures for strategy implementation are provided in the delivery (D) section. References and/or other resources are provided at the end of each strategy description.

A graphic at the beginning of each strategy identifies the time when the strategy should be used (before, during, or after reading), the most appropriate group size (one-on-one, small group, or whole group), and the grade levels for which the strategy would be most applicable (PreK–2, 3–5, 6–8). Although the designation of before, during, and/or after reading is often used when talking about direct interaction with a text, we also use it to identify where the strategy might be used during a lesson that spans more than just the reading of a text. In addition, it is important to note that grade-level designations can vary based on the developmental levels of students. Almost all strategies can be modified and used at different points in the reading process and with a variety of group sizes and grade levels, so the information identified in the graphic should be viewed as flexible.

When to Teach		Group Size		Grade Level	
Before Reading		One-on-One		PreK–2	
During Reading		Small Group		3–5	
After Reading		Whole Group		6–8	

Although the strategies are organized around specific literacy areas, many of them can be used in multiple areas.

References

International Reading Association. 2000. *Excellent reading teachers* a position statement. Retrieved March 10, 2008, from http://www.reading.org/.
National Reading Panel. 2000. *Teaching children to read: An evidence-based assessment of the scientific research literature on reading and its implications for reading instruction* (NIH Publication No. 00-4769). Washington, DC: National Institute of Child Health and Human Development, National Institutes of Health.

Dedication

With much love we dedicate this book
to our families, with special appreciation to certain young ones.

To my brilliant, beautiful daughters—Reghan Valerie and Kendall
Maureen. You have both been gifted with extraordinary teachers
throughout your whole lives, and I am grateful for the lessons you
have learned and continue to learn from them. As you develop
as lifelong learners, I want you to remember this quotation from
C. S. Lewis: "You are never too old to set another goal or to
dream a new dream."

KK-L

To my two beautiful grandchildren, who
are just now entering the world of "formal" education.
May you enjoy many years of learning in the care of
passionate, dedicated, and high-quality strategic teachers.
Thanks, Kelcey and Brason, for understanding why Mema
was so busy all those weekends—I love you both!

CLC

Section I

Oral Language

Oral language is the ability to express oneself verbally and is the foundation for strong literacy instruction (Cummins and Stewart 2006). Even though the National Reading Panel report (2000) did not identify oral language as one of the essential elements of reading instruction, many studies emphasize the high priority of oral language development (e.g., Dickinson and Snow 1987; Hart and Risley 1995; Purcell-Gates 1988). Oral language development focuses on the development of spoken language, including listening and speaking. Researchers have concluded that reading is a language process, so it must be closely associated with oral language (Morrow 2001, 92). To help students become readers, we must expand our knowledge of oral language development and the ways in which it can make the connection between the spoken word and written word.

Our goal as teachers should be to encourage language use across a variety of contexts. After all, "oral language is not just a subject, but the means by which all other subjects are pursued" (Traill 2003). It is important that "oral language and communication experiences should take center stage in the primary classroom" (Soderman, Gregory, and O'Neill 1999, 97). One way to encourage oral language in the classroom is to create social situations in which students can interact with other students and adults. This can be accomplished by providing students with a wide array of literacy activities, in which they can have new experiences and can share and discuss these experiences with each other throughout the school day. Short turn and talks at strategic points in the lesson provide students with opportunities to share their thinking while practicing the use of language. Other suggested ways to develop oral language in the classroom include:

- Storytelling activities as a way to orally present a story. The story can be told so that listeners learn about particular traditions that are embedded in the story.
- Puppets, puppet theaters, or other story props when retelling a story.
- Songs and music for students to sing along with the words. The words can be displayed on chart paper for students to see as they sing.
- Poetry verses with which students can sing, chant, or provide movement as they read the lines of text.
- Activities in which students engage in talk with each other about what they are learning or reading.
- Word play in which students explore the rhythmic aspects of language, such as identifying rhyming words.
- Role-playing activities in which students act out stories they have read in class. Classrooms should have a center area where students role-play what people do in the kitchen or other parts of the house, a post office, a store, or other types of areas they may visit.
- Reading aloud to students from a variety of books from different types of genres.
- Integrated language development strategies throughout the day, such as barrier games, grand conversations, and sketch-to-stretch.

Oral language instruction is sometimes overlooked or underestimated by teachers (Cummins and Stewart 2006). It is often assumed that oral language will simply develop from exposure. However, oral language development requires the same purposeful planning and explicit instruction as other elements of literacy instruction. It is the teacher's job to provide experiences through which students can build and expand their use of language. When teachers take time to build oral language skills, they are helping readers learn how to communicate more effectively as they learn to listen and speak with each other. This foundation supplied by oral language will help students to be more successful as they learn to read and write.

References

Cummins, C., and M. Stewart. (2006). Oral language: A strong foundation for literacy instruction. *In understanding and implementing reading first initiatives*, 90–105. Newark, DE: International Reading Association.

Dickinson, D. K., and C. E. Snow. 1987. Interrelationships between prereading and oral language skills in kindergartners from two social classes. *Early Childhood Research Quarterly* 2: 1–25.

Hart, B., and T. R. Risley. 1995. *Meaningful differences in the everyday experience of young American children*. Baltimore: Paul H. Brookes.

Morrow, L. M. (2001). Literacy development in the early years: Helping children learn to read and write (4th Ed.). Needham Heights, MA: Allyn & Bacon.

National Reading Panel. 2000. *Teaching children to read: An evidence-based assessment of the scientific research literature on reading and its implications for reading instruction* (NIH Publication No. 00-4769). Washington, DC: National Institute of Child Health and Human Development, National Institutes of Health.

Purcell-Gates, V. 1988. Lexical and syntactic knowledge of written narrative held by well-read-to kindergartners and second graders. *Research in the Teaching of English* 22: 128–60.

Soderman, A. K., K. M. Gregory, and L. T. O'Neill. 1999. *Scaffolding emergent literacy: A child-centered approach for preschool through grade 5*. Needham Heights, MA: Allyn & Bacon.

Traill, L. 2003, December. *Trails to literacy: Improving literacy achievement schoolwide*. Preconference institute presentation, Louisiana Reading Association, Baton Rouge, LA.

BARRIER GAMES

When to Teach		Group Size		Grade Level	
Before Reading	📖	One-on-One	👥	PreK–2	🏫
During Reading		Small Group	👥	3–5	🏫
After Reading	📖	Whole Group		6–8	🏫

R–Rationale

Even though barrier games are not directly related to reading, they provide practice in using decontextualized language precisely, which helps students develop skills needed for learning to read. This strategy provides teacher guidance as students have an opportunity for extended talk (Kotler, Wegerif, and LeVoi 2001).

E–Explanation

Barrier games are activities that require players to give precise and explicit instructions/descriptions and to listen attentively. A barrier is placed between the players so that neither can see what the other is doing. One student orally describes the steps of a task or describes an object so that the player on the other side of the barrier can complete the actions or identify the item. The game usually requires two players but can be done with a small group of three to five students.

Barrier games encourage students to practice using precise language in order to adequately convey their thoughts to a listener. These games can involve a variety of activities such as describing an object, drawing an object, or reading a series of directions:

- Describing an object involves one student in selecting a small object from a bag or a collection of items and describing it to another student. The second student must listen attentively in order to guess the object.
- Drawing an object requires Student A to describe a picture or illustration to Student B without identifying the object represented in the illustration. Student B draws the object, based on the information received from Student A. When the drawing is complete, the barrier is removed, and the two pictures compared.
- Following directions is another form of barrier game. A set of directions is printed on index cards, such as "Place a red dot next to the green tree. Draw a blue circle around the red dot." Student A reads the directions to Student B, who completes the actions described. Students can also be given identical maps; Student A charts a course on his map and then gives directions to Student B to trace the same course.

Even though barrier games are not directly related to reading, they can be modified to work with stories. One player chooses a specific action or event from a story and provides an explicit description from which the other player has to identify the action or event being described.

A–Application

The teacher arranges the class into two-member groups by sliding desks together so the students can face each other. A trifolded manila folder is placed between the students as a barrier. One student selects an object from the mystery bag and returns to her desk, hiding the object behind the barrier so the other student cannot see it. The teacher reminds the students that all directions/descriptions have to be given orally. The students then describe their objects to their partners, sharing characteristics until the Item is identified. Students then reverse roles.

D–Delivery

Barrier games are easy to set up and can take on a variety of formats. Each type of game should first be modeled by the teacher prior to students playing independently.

1. The teacher selects the type of barrier game to be played.
2. A barrier is placed between the two players so that neither can see what the other is doing.
3. One player takes the lead and gives the oral description of the object, the directions to be followed, the steps to be completed, and so on, while the other player listens and attempts to complete the task.
4. The barrier is removed, and the results checked for accuracy.

Reference

Kotler, A., R. Wegerif, and M. LeVoi, 2001. Oracy and the educational achievement of pupils with English as an additional language: The impact of bringing "talking partners" into Bradford schools. *International Journal of Bilingual Education and Bilingualism* 4: 403–19.

DIRECTED LISTENING–THINKING ACTIVITY

When to Teach		Group Size		Grade Level	
Before Reading	📖	One-on-One	👥	PreK–2	🏫
During Reading	📖	Small Group	👥	3–5	🏫
After Reading	📖	Whole Group	👥	6–8	🏫

R–Rationale

A directed listening–thinking activity (DL–TA) helps students to build on knowledge they already have and make connections to new information. Adapted from Stauffer's directed reading–thinking activity (1969), this type of activity is intended to elicit students' prior knowledge about a text, set a purpose for reading, and then help students learn how to monitor their comprehension as the text is being read. This type of activity is also beneficial in helping to develop and reinforce oral language, since students are able to talk with the teacher and each other as they explore their ideas about the text. In addition, such an activity helps to build a bridge between what students talk about and what they will later read and write. It is important not to be deceived by the listening part of DL–TA; it also involves students in thinking and speaking with the teacher and each other as they make sense of what they have read. Teachers can easily use either fiction or nonfiction texts for the DL–TA.

E–Explanation

The DL–TA is very similar to a read-aloud except that it is more structured in the cycle that is followed: students are involved in making predictions, listening to the teacher read a segment of the story aloud, talking about the text, and then making new predictions. The cycle of making predictions, listening, reviewing, and revising predictions continues until the story is finished.

A–Application

The teacher reads the title of the book, *Bubushka's Doll* by Patricia Polacco, aloud to students and tells them it is about a little girl who learns a lesson from a doll. Students are asked to brainstorm what they think might happen, based on this overview. The teacher writes each idea down on chart paper, chalkboard, or projection system. Next, the teacher reads aloud two to three pages of the book while also showing students the pictures. The teacher should pause after the first segment of text and refer students to the ideas that were listed on the chart paper. The teacher asks students if any of the ideas seem more likely to occur, what they think will happen next, and whether they have changed their predictions about what will happen in the story. The teacher records any new predictions on the chart paper, then continues reading the book in two- to three-page segments until the story is completed. The teacher should be sure to pause after each segment is read to ask students if they have changed their minds about what they think will happen next in the story. The teacher should also encourage students to explain why they have changed their predictions by referring to examples in the story.

D–Delivery

The DL–TA involves a cycle of making predictions, reading a segment of text, reviewing what was predicted, then making new predictions based on the new information.

1. Introduce the story by identifying the title and author.
2. Show students the first page of the book. Examine the pictures and talk about what clues students can gather about the story from the pictures.
3. Ask students to make predictions about what they think will happen in the story, based on their review of the title, cover, and first picture.
4. Write down all predictions on chart paper, chalkboard, or projection system.
5. Read a short segment of text aloud to students. For picture books, this page length may be anywhere from two to five, depending on how much text is on the page. For beginning chapter books, novels, or nonfiction texts, the number of pages read can be two to three.
6. Pause after the segment is read, and revisit the predictions that were written down on the chart paper. Ask students if any of these predictions seem likely to occur or not occur.
7. Ask students to make new predictions based on the new information they heard in the story. Write these new predictions down on the chart paper.
8. Continue this cycle until the book is finished.
9. After reading, take time to discuss the story with students.

References

Polacco, P. 1995. *Babushka's doll*. New York: Simon & Schuster.
Stauffer, R. G. 1969. *Directing reading maturity as a cognitive process*. New York: Harper & Row.

ELABORATION

When to Teach		Group Size		Grade Level	
Before Reading	📖	One-on-One	👥	PreK–2	🏫
During Reading		Small Group	👥	3–5	🏫
After Reading	📖	Whole Group		6–8	🏫

R–Rationale

Elaboration (Beck, McKeown, and Kucan 2002) is an oral language strategy designed to extend the level of language used by students–both the level of communication and the level of vocabulary. Students need to participate in conversations that move beyond yes/no or short-answer responses. Elaboration allows the conversation to go back and forth, with the teacher pushing the level of thought with each interchange.

E–Explanation

Elaboration is similar to what Bruner (1978) described mothers doing to extend their children's language. This extended discourse allows teachers to elaborate their conversations with students or conversations among students, while providing an opportunity for the students to go beyond the immediate issue. This form of productive talk not only improves oral language skills but also builds vocabulary.

A–Application

While taking the morning roll, the teacher notices that one student appears to be bored. After completing the roll, the teacher encounters the student, and the following exchange takes place:

> *Teacher:* Good morning, Mason. What's on your mind?
> *Student:* Nothing, I can just tell that it is going to be a dull day.
> *Teacher:* What would make it not a dull day, perhaps even an exciting day?
> *Student:* I guess if we could work in the science center, then it wouldn't be a dull day.
> *Teacher:* Would that make it an exciting day?
> *Student:* Yes, that would be exciting.
> *Teacher:* Well, what could make it more than exciting, maybe spectacular?
> *Student:* If we had recess all day.
> *Teacher:* So are you saying that having recess all day wouldn't be dull but would be exciting or even spectacular?
> *Student:* Yes, that would be exciting, I mean spectacular.

The teacher realized that the conversation did require a little time but that the extended dialogue not only engaged the student in using communicative language but also extended his vocabulary (and maybe even helped him not be too bored).

D–Delivery

There are no step-by-step procedures for using elaboration in the classroom; however, there are a few principles that will enhance implementation:

1. Pay attention to conversations between student and teacher and among students in order to take advantage of a teachable moment in which to extend the students' language.
2. Be cautious in responding with simple yes or no answers or answers that basically cut off conversation.
3. Respond by asking questions that not only probe a student's understanding but also offer other words or concepts that push the student's thinking and/or vocabulary and language knowledge.
4. Be careful of your body language while conversing with students. They can quickly pick up on signs that you are not interested in what they are saying and will then be reluctant to continue the conversation.
5. Remember that even though you are trying to push a student's use of language, you do not want to dominate the conversation. Teachers should talk only enough to keep the dialogue flowing at a more critical level.

References

Beck, I. L., M. G. McKeown, and L. Kucan. 2002. *Bringing words to life: Robust vocabulary instruction*. New York: Guilford.

Bruner, J. S. 1978. The role of dialogue in language acquisition. In *The child's conception of language*, ed. A. Sinclair, R. J. Jarvella, and W. J. M. Levelt, 241–56. Berlin, Germany: Springer-Verlag.

GRAND CONVERSATIONS

When to Teach		Group Size		Grade Level	
Before Reading		One-on-One		PreK–2	🏫
During Reading		Small Group	👥	3–5	🏫
After Reading	📖	Whole Group	👥	6–8	🏫

R–Rationale

Grand conversations are designed to help students and the teacher coproduce meaning as they take up one another's ideas, add to them, and move them to higher levels. Grand conversations help build language, flexibility of mind, and consideration of alternate viewpoints.

E–Explanation

Grand conversations (Peterson and Eeds 1990) are give-and-take discussions in which the partners in a dialogue depend on one another's ideas and encouragement to keep the conversation moving. A grand conversation usually develops around a particular class theme. It might be a group inquiry session built around a piece of literature that the class has read or heard or even a topic that has been studied. It is very similar to an instructional conversation, with the primary difference being that grand conversations generally evolve around narrative texts, and instructional conversations around informational texts.

A–Application

After reading the story "Jack and the Beanstalk", a group of second graders share key things they liked and disliked about the story. Following the discussion, the teacher sets the stage for deeper conversation by asking the class if they thought this was a good story for young students. The following conversation was elicited after students listened to the story and created a class big book (Cherry 1995, p. 4).

> *Ranea:* I don't think this story is good. It has stealing, lying, and killing in it.
> *Tom:* Yea, some kids might get bad ideas from reading it.
> *Shandra:* I liked some of the story. I liked the part that Jack and his wife lived happily ever after.
> *Ranea:* It could be good to read the story to kids. Maybe they could learn something from it like to never steal or lie.

D–Delivery

A grand conversation can vary, depending on the group and the topic being discussed, but generally an inquiry session proceeds as follows:

1. Students read or listen to a story (in sections if a lengthy text).
2. The teacher and students sit in a large circle, facing each other. When the process is first initiated, the teacher might want to have students share their ideas about the text in small groups before bringing the conversation to the entire class. This is especially helpful when students are hesitant to talk.
3. Someone, usually the teacher initially, starts the conversation by asking, "What did you think?"
4. After a short open discussion, the students move to more thoughtful, open-ended questions until someone initiates an idea or a stance on an issue.
5. Students defend the stance or respond to the questions based on personal beliefs, information from the story, and various other perspectives.
6. Students take turns talking about the idea introduced by the speaker until the idea is exhausted.
7. A student then introduces a new idea, and students discuss it until it is exhausted. It is important to note that only one idea is discussed at a time and the teacher should remain as silent as possible. It is also important that comments from a specific student be limited so that everyone can participate.
8. If needed, the teacher may ask questions that focus students' attention on an aspect of the text that has been missed or on a specific area or task (e.g., an element of story structure, author's craft, comparison of an event to one in another book, or a moral from the story).
9. The teacher closes the conversation by summarizing it, drawing conclusions from it, and so on.
10. Students may also reflect on the conversation via writing.

References

Cherry, M. T. 1995. Class big book, "Jack and the beanstalk". Unpublished raw data.
Peterson, R. I., and M. Eeds. 1990. *Grand conversations*. New York: Scholastic.

LANGUAGE EXPERIENCE APPROACH

When to Teach		Group Size		Grade Level	
Before Reading	📖	One-on-One	👥	PreK–2	🏫
During Reading		Small Group		3–5	
After Reading	📖	Whole Group		6–8	

R–Rationale

The language experience approach (LEA) gives students opportunities to explore reading and writing using texts they have composed based on their own experiences. It provides them with many opportunities to see, react, think, speak, be listened to, read, and share (Stauffer 1980). The LEA also provides reading material that is predictable and readable because it uses the learners' natural language.

E–Explanation

The LEA is an approach to reading instruction that is based on activities and stories developed from the personal experiences of the learners. The stories about personal experiences are written down by a teacher and read together until the learners associate the written form of the word with the spoken form of the word. The most common approach is for students to share an experience and dictate a story about the experience to the teacher, who then writes it down so that the students can read and reread the text. The LEA helps to teach students in the primary grades not only reading but also the process of writing by showing them that what they say can be written down and read back. Again, the key with the LEA is that the language of the children must be written down "as is," because when the children read it back, it will be that language that is used.

A–Application

The teacher and students go for a walk around the playground. After returning to the classroom, the teacher talks with the students about what happened during the walk. The students then dictate a story that tells what happened while on the walk. The teacher writes down, on chart paper exactly what the students say, using their language as often as possible. Each time a new sentence is composed, the teacher pauses and rereads what has been recorded for the story up until that point. Once the story is completed, the teacher helps the students read the story several times. The teacher then posts the story on the wall so that the students can read it as desired.

D–Delivery

The LEA gives students multiple opportunities to explore language.

1. Provide an experience for students that will serve as the basis for the LEA.

2. Talk about the experience together to help the students review what happened. This process helps familiarize students with key vocabulary words that they will use when they dictate their narrative of the experience.
3. Guide this discussion by asking questions that help students reflect on the experience.
4. After the discussion, have students dictate their story to you. Write the story on a large piece of chart paper (or notepaper if doing the activity with one child), using the students' words as much as possible.
5. Stop periodically to read aloud what has been written so far. Point to the words during the reading of the story.
6. Once the story is completed, read back the entire story, pointing to the words again to track the print.
7. Encourage the students to reread the story several times, both with your support and on their own.

Reference

Stauffer, R. G. 1980. *The language experience approach to the teaching of reading*. New York: Harper & Row.

RETELLING

When to Teach		Group Size		Grade Level	
Before Reading		One-on-One	👥	PreK–2	🏫
During Reading		Small Group	👥	3–5	🏫
After Reading	📖	Whole Group		6–8	🏫

R–Rationale

Research confirms that retelling improves comprehension, concept of story, critical thinking, and oral language development (Hu 1995; Koskinen et al. 1988). When used to encourage dialogue about a story, it is probably one of the most comprehensive strategies for developing oral language because it requires students to use a multitude of expressive verbal skills.

E–Explanation

Retelling is not just a short-term recall of all that students can remember from a story but rather is the students' construction of meaning (Benson and Cummins 2000). It is a reflection of their understanding of the text. This is a complex task as it requires the readers not only to understand what they have read but to then put their understanding into oral language. The complexity of this task requires the teacher to scaffold the activity. Initially, the teacher models how to retell the story and slowly invites the students to join in. It is important that the teacher uses her own words in retelling and not the words of the author, or students may think they have to memorize the story. Illustrations, story props, and graphic organizers can be used one at a time to support the students as they mature in their retellings. The use of these items frees the students from trying to remember all of the details of the story so they can focus on the language needed to put the story in their own words as they share it with others. It is important that the teacher models retelling using each of these mediums several times before students are expected to use them as an aid in their own retellings.

It is important to note that retelling differs from summarization, which requires readers to produce a condensed representation of the general gist of the story. Retelling, on the other hand, requires readers not only to recall information from the story but to basically recreate the story in their own words. Even though they do not have to recall everything from the story, they should include all of the elements of the story, using their own language.

A–Application

After reading the story *The Pesky Paua* (Cunningham 1992), the teacher works with a small group of second-grade students to model how to retell the story using illustrations. The teacher covers the text using office correction and cover tape so that students' attention is not drawn to the text. The teacher then opens to the first page, looks at the illustration on the page, and begins to retell the story in his own words.

> Annie was at the beach looking for paua, which is a kind of shellfish. She looked everywhere but only found little ones that needed to be left alone so they could grow bigger. All of a sudden, Annie saw the biggest paua she had ever seen.

The teacher continues retelling the story using the illustrations on each page to model how to recall events while keeping the whole story in mind. The teacher then gives the book to the students so they can use the illustrations to retell the story to each other.

D–Delivery

Providing step-by-step procedures for the retelling strategy is almost impossible because it requires many steps to scaffold students into effective retellings. However, the following might serve as supportive steps in guiding students to independent retellings:

1. Teachers should model retelling before asking students to do an independent retelling. After reading a story to the class, the teacher retells the story, paying attention to the progress from the beginning to the end of the story and using the teacher's own words rather than those of the author. This should continue until the teacher feels that students understand the concept of retelling.
2. When students first begin to retell independently, they need as much support as possible; allowing them to use the illustrations of the story while retelling it provides this support. The book itself can be used for this purpose, but the text should be covered (correction and cover-up tape works well) so that students do not attempt to read the text rather than retelling it.
3. Once students have become proficient retellers using illustrations, some of the support should be relinquished. Story props provide some support but not as much as illustrations. The teacher should select props that represent the key elements of the story rather than simply all characters. The props do not have to be directly from the story but should be representative of the setting, character, key events, and so on.
4. Once students can retell with story props, they are ready to move to more generalized props (e.g., story hand, graphic organizer, shape map) and then finally to retelling without visual support.
5. It is important to remember that at each developmental stage, the teacher should model retelling using that level of support so that students understand how to use the support to guide their retelling.

References

Benson, V., and C. Cummins. 2000. *The power of retelling: Developmental steps for building comprehension.* Bothell, WA: Wright Group/McGraw-Hill.
Cunningham, R. 1992. *The pesky paua.* Petone, New Zealand: Nelson Price Milburn.
Hu, H. 1995. Bringing written retelling into an ESL English as a second language writing class. *Journal of Developmental Education* 19 (1): 12–14.
Koskinen, P. S., L. B. Gambrell, B. A. Kapinus, and B. S. Heathington. 1988. Retelling: A strategy of enhancing students' reading comprehension. *The Reading Teacher* 41: 892–96.

ROLE PLAY

When to Teach		Group Size		Grade Level	
Before Reading		One-on-One	📖	PreK–2	🏫
During Reading		Small Group	👥	3–5	
After Reading	📖	Whole Group		6–8	

R–Rationale

Role-playing allows opportunities for students to put their thoughts into words without the fear of being right or wrong. It also helps students to become aware of other people's feelings and to rehearse the social interactions the students may encounter with friends. Role-playing gives students an opportunity to modify their actions in order to emulate the person or character they are portraying.

E–Explanation

Role-play is an opportunity for students to express themselves in roles other than their own. Because students naturally use stories they have heard in their play activities at school, role-playing is an excellent way to encourage dialogue about a story. Role-playing can be left entirely to the children or can include the teacher through various degrees of involvement (Campbell 2001). The teacher can assist students in conducting a dramatized version of a story or leave the children to role-play together. Props are not necessary, yet a designated space for an imaginative setting facilitates the role-playing. A versatile and flexible structure for this activity results when a pole is added to each end of a bookcase. Between the tops of the two poles, teachers can attach a rod on which a divided curtain can be hung so that a movable "stage" is available for use as a puppet stage, a reception desk, a doctor's office, a principal's office, a grocery store, or other imaginative setting. In addition to role-playing characters or events from a story read, students can take the role of another person in the class, a movie, the community, and so forth. They can even play themselves.

A–Application

After reading the story *Berenstain Bears Visit the Dentist* (Berenstain and Berenstain 1981), a small group of first-grade students get together to discuss the story. The children decide that they want to pretend that they are going to the dentist. One child decides to be the dentist, one the patient, and the two other students are patients waiting to see the dentist. The patients in the waiting room quickly go to the reading center and bring back several books to read and talk about while they wait. The other students pull a chair away from the table to serve as the dental chair. The student patient has a seat and waits for the dentist. When the dentist arrives, he quickly has the patient open her mouth and stick out her tongue, and he then begins to make a growling sound as he pretends to drill in her mouth. The patient appropriately moans. The dentist then scribbles something on a sheet of paper, hands it to the patient, and says, "Go to the drugstore and get this filled, and you'll feel better."

D–Delivery

Role-play is a very open-ended oral language strategy and does not lend itself to a step delivery model. However, when planning role-playing activities, teachers should keep the following in mind:

1. The roles students choose to play are usually not well defined by adult standards. Students need freedom in defining the roles to fit their needs.
2. The roles might change throughout the activity. Students often move back and forth in different roles during an activity.
3. It is not necessary to have elaborate props for the role-play; however, a designated space for an imaginative setting does facilitate the role-playing.
4. Students can role-play a variety of things: characters or events from a story, a friend, the teacher, a community helper, an event they have been involved in, or even a stuffed animal. The door should remain open for their imagination: it is not the role-playing that is important but the opportunity it gives students to use language.

References

Berenstain, S., and J. Berenstain. 1981. *Berenstain Bears Visit the Dentist*. New York: Random House.
Campbell, R. 2001. *Read-alouds with young children*. Newark, DE: International Reading Association.

SKETCH-TO-STRETCH

When to Teach		Group Size		Grade Level	
Before Reading		One-on-One		PreK–2	
During Reading		Small Group		3–5	
After Reading		Whole Group		6–8	

R–Rationale

Sketch-to-stretch (Harste, Short, and Burke 1988) is a strategy that encourages students to monitor their comprehension as they process what they read. It also fosters students' listening skills while engaging their verbal/linguistic, visual/spatial, interpersonal, and intrapersonal intelligences.

E–Explanation

Sketch-to-stretch is an extension activity in which students quickly draw a sketch that represents what the story or section of a story means to them. The strategy can be used at the completion of a reading assignment but is usually more beneficial when done at various points during the reading. Generally the strategy includes both a listening and a reading task but can be done strictly as a listening activity or as a reading assignment.

A–Application

The teacher introduces the book *Goldilocks and the Three Bears* (Brett 1992) to the class by sharing the title and cover. Students think about the clues provided and write a prediction on their sketch-to-stretch chart. The teacher then reads the story up to the point when the three bears go for a walk in the woods. The students quickly make a sketch representing their understanding of the text up to this point. Students then do a turn-and-talk and share their illustrations, paying attention to the key points that led them to what they drew. Next, these key points are recorded in the summary section beside the drawing. The teacher then continues reading until the next key sketching point arrives and the process is repeated.

D–Delivery

Sketch-to-stretch provides insight into students' understanding of a text but more importantly into their thinking and interpretation of the text.

1. Pass out copies of the sketch-to-stretch chart, or have students divide a sheet of paper into two boxes for each section to be read.

2. Read the title of the selection aloud. Have students write what they already know about the topic in the prediction box at the top of the chart.
3. Read one section of the selection aloud, and ask students to sketch in the first box what comes to mind as they listen.
4. After students complete their sketch, distribute copies of the text for students to read. Advise students to revise their drawings by adding details as needed.
5. When their drawings are complete, ask students to pair off and talk about their sketches, explaining what they were thinking about as they drew. Tell pairs to come to a consensus on what is important to remember from the text they listened to and read.
6. Have students summarize these important points in the box next to each drawing.
7. Repeat this sequence with either the teacher reading sections of the text and then students rereading or students proceeding on their own until the reading selection is complete.
8. The discussion can be extended to include a conversation about the different ideas the students had about the story.

References

Brett, J. 1992. *Goldilocks and the three bears*. New York: Putnam.

Harste, J., K. Short, and C. Burke. 1988. *Creating classrooms for authors*. Portsmouth, NH: Heinemann.

SKETCH-TO-STRETCH

Prediction

Sketch	Summary of Important Points
Sketch	Summary of Important Points
Sketch	Summary of Important Points

Section II
Phonemic Awareness

Phonemes are the smallest units of spoken language, and phonemic awareness is the ability to hear, identify, and manipulate the sounds in spoken words. A child is able to hear the differences between similar words—say, *cup* and *cut*—in natural speech long before entering the school setting (Clay 1979). But the child may not know that these two words each consist of three sounds, with the ending sound being the main difference between the two words. Before students learn to read print, they need to become aware that words are made up of speech sounds, or phonemes, and they need to know how the sounds in words work.

Phonemic awareness is a widely used and often misunderstood reading term—it is not phonics. Phonemic awareness involves being able to say a word aloud, recognize that the word is made up of sounds, segment the sounds and blend them back together, and manipulate sounds to make new words. A larger, more encompassing term is *phonological awareness*, which includes phonemic awareness as well as awareness of larger spoken units. Phonological awareness is the broad class of skills that involves attending to, thinking about, and intentionally manipulating the phonological aspects of written language (Scarborough and Brady 2002), including such things as rhymes, words, syllables, and onsets and rimes (Armbruster, Lehr, and Osborn 2001).

Students who can hear the sounds in words will later be able to make sense of the letters they encounter in words. Activities that help to develop phonological awareness include playing with rhymes, working with onset and rime, and practicing segmenting words. These types of tasks are easier for beginning readers than those that require specific areas of phonemic awareness: blending, segmenting, and manipulating. The tasks involved in phonological awareness vary in difficulty. According to Dechant (1993), there are three levels of phonological awareness, each involving three awareness tasks:

Level *One*
1. *Awareness of gross differences:* Recognizing that words represent a sound unit-word awareness.
2. *Awareness of rhyme:* Hearing and recognizing rhymes.
3. *Segmentation of words into syllables:* Detecting that words are made up of different part-syllables.

Level *Two*
4. *Awareness of initial consonant segments:* Generating a word that has a given sound at the beginning, middle, or end.
5. *Alliteration:* Identifying words that have a given sound.
6. *Awareness/segmentation of onset and rime:* Hearing and manipulating the onset and rime of words.

Level *Three*
7. *Phonemic segmentation:* Isolating sounds at the beginning of a word or in an entire word. Sometimes the task requires hearing and counting; at other times it requires producing the actual sound.
8. *Blending of phonemes and syllables:* Putting sounds together to form a word.
9. *Phonemic manipulation:* Substituting, adding, or deleting sounds to create new words.

Levels 1 and 2 deal with larger units of sounds, Level 3 represents phonemic awareness as students begin to segment, blend, and manipulate individual phonemes.

The important point to remember is that phonological awareness can be taught and that students who increase their awareness of phonemes facilitate their subsequent reading acquisition (Spector 1995). Effective phonemic awareness instruction positively affects reading acquisition and spelling (Ehri et al. 2001) and "teaches children to notice, think about, and work with (manipulate) sounds in spoken language" (Armbruster, Lehr, and Osborn 2001, 5).

Findings from the National Reading Panel report indicate that phonemic awareness instruction is more effective when students are taught to apply the skills in phonemic awareness to reading and writing and to focus on one to two types of phoneme manipulation rather than multiple types. In addition, instruction is more effective when students are taught in small groups (NICHD 2000).

References

Armbruster, B. B., F. Lehr, and J. Osborn. 2001. *Put reading first: The research building blocks for teaching children to read*. Jessup, MD: National Institute for Literacy.

Clay, M. M. 1979. *Reading: The patterning of complex behavior*. Portsmouth, NH: Heinemann.

Dechant, E. 1993. Cited in S. Forbes, L. Gray, and N. Bankson, Schools teaching early phonological awareness skills: Phonological awareness in preschool. Retrieved August 27, 2008, from *http://www.doe.virginia.gov/VDOE/Instruction/Reading/doe-pa.pdf*.

Ehri, L. C., S. Nunes, S. Stahl, and D. Willows. 2001. Systematic phonics instruction helps students learn to read: Evidence from the National Reading Panel's meta-analysis. *Review of Educational Research* 71, 393–47.

National Reading Panel. 2000. *Teaching children to read: An evidence-based assessment of the scientific research literature on reading and its implications for reading instruction* (NIH Publication No. 00-4769). Washington, DC: National Institute of Child Health and Human Development, National Institutes of Health.

Scarborough, H. S., and S. A. Brady. 2002. Toward a common terminology for talking about speech and reading: A glossary of the "phon" words and some related terms. *Journal of Literacy Research* 34, 299–36.

Spector, J. E. 1995. Phonemic awareness training: Application of principles of direct instruction. *Reading and Writing Quarterly: Overcoming Language Difficulties* 11 (1): 37–52.

CLAPPING SYLLABLES

When to Teach		Group Size		Grade Level	
Before Reading		One-on-One		PreK–2	
During Reading		Small Group		3–5	
After Reading		Whole Group		6–8	

R–Rationale

Clapping syllables is an activity that focuses students' attention on the number of syllables they hear in words. Students who are able to attend to and think about phonological aspects of written language, such as the syllables in words, will later be able to make sense of the letters they encounter in words (Armbruster, Lehr, and Osborn 2001).

E–Explanation

Students clap their hands, tap the desk, or snap their fingers as they break a word into syllables. Being able to hear the syllables in words is a precursor to being able to break the word down further into individual sounds.

A–Application

As with any new skill, it is important to model how to do it before asking students to do it by themselves. Teachers can easily model the process of clapping the number of syllables that are heard in words. Begin by pronouncing a word, such as *airplane*. Next, say the word aloud again as the syllables are clapped (*air-plane*). Invite students to say the word as everyone claps the syllables together (*air-plane*). Repeat this process with other words, such as *monkey*, *hot*, *chalkboard*, *notebook*, and *cat*. Remind students to listen carefully, since the words might have one or two syllables. A variation is to ask students to say a word without one of its syllables. For example, say the word *rooster* without the *-ster*. This requires more cognitive processing on the part of the students and should not be done until students are able to easily count the syllables they hear in words.

D–Delivery

It is best to start with two-syllable words when clapping the syllables that are heard in words. Once students have shown that they are able to clap for two-syllable words, then students can progress to three-syllable words.

1. Pronounce a word aloud.
2. Repeat the word while clapping the syllables.

3. Ask students to say the word with you as you clap the syllables.
4. Repeat this process with several different words.
5. Once students understand how the process works, pronounce the word and clap the syllables together.
6. As students become more proficient, they can take turns clapping the syllables with a partner or a small group of students.

Reference

Armbruster, B. B., F. Lehr, and J. Osborn 2001. *Put reading first: The research building blocks for teaching children to read*. Jessup, MD: National Institute for Literacy.

ELKONIN BOXES

When to Teach		Group Size		Grade Level	
Before Reading		One-on-One		PreK–2	
During Reading		Small Group		3–5	
After Reading		Whole Group		6–8	

R–Rationale

Elkonin boxes (Elkonin 1973) help make the abstractness of hearing individual phonemes (sounds) in a word more concrete for students by actively engaging their motor skills in addition to their listening. It is a strategy that is used to teach students to segment words.

E–Explanation

Elkonin boxes are a simple device that provides a concrete, hands-on way for students to practice and demonstrate their ability to hear individual sounds in words. With this strategy, a child views pictures of objects with squares below the pictures corresponding to the number of sounds in the word. The child places a counter in the appropriate square as each sound is made.

   The strategy can also be used without pictures: the teacher can say the word, and students can slide a counter into the appropriate box as each sound is heard.
   If students have already moved into phonics and know the letters that correspond to the sounds, magnetic letters can be used in lieu of markers. For example, the teacher would say bat, and students would slide the magnetic letters b-a-t into the appropriate box.

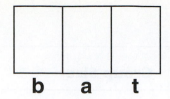

b a t

A–Application

The teacher gives the students three to four pictures of objects with squares below each picture to represent the sounds in each word. The teacher models how the task should be done by doing the first picture for the students. The teacher pronounces the word *dog,* slowly drawing out the sounds. As the /d/ sound is made, the teacher places the counter in the first square. Another counter is placed in the next square as the /ŏ/ sound is made, and a counter is placed in the third square as the /g/ sound is made. If the students are having difficulty, the teacher continues to model and lead through the rest of the activity. Otherwise, the students can complete the activity either independently or in small groups—pronouncing the name of each object slowly, separating each sound, and placing a counter in the corresponding square.

D–Delivery

Elkonin boxes help students learn to segment sounds in words. The boxes and markers provide a concrete hands-on way for students to practice and demonstrate their ability to hear individual sounds in words.

1. The teacher draws a rectangle divided into small boxes on a strip of paper; the number of boxes should match the number of phonemes in the words the students will be listening to.
2. The teacher gives each student an Elkonin box and markers (counters, paper, candy); the number of markers should correspond to the number of squares in the Elkonin box.
3. The teacher pronounces a word slowly, stretching it out (i.e., turtle talk).
4. Students repeat the word slowly, listening for the number of sounds they hear.
5. Students then repeat the word again, this time sliding a marker into a box for each sound heard.
6. Students slide a finger below each marker as they once again say the word.

References

Elkonin, D. B. 1973. Reading in the USSR. In *Comparative reading*, ed. J. Downing, 551–79. New York: Macmillan.
Clay, M. M. 1979. *Reading: The patterning of complex behavior*. Portsmouth, NH: Heinemann.

LANGUAGE PLAY

When to Teach		Group Size		Grade Level	
Before Reading		One-on-One		PreK–2	
During Reading		Small Group		3–5	
After Reading		Whole Group		6–8	

R–Rationale

Language play, or word play as it is sometimes called, contributes to an understanding of the technical aspects of language, strengthens listening and reading skills, and extends vocabulary. Teachers can use students' natural love of language to create a learning environment that facilitates language acquisition.

E–Explanation

Jongsma (2000) points out that the building blocks of the English language are the eight parts of speech—nouns, verbs, adjectives, adverbs, pronouns, conjunctions, prepositions, and interjections. She contends that these parts of speech are filled with wonderful sounds that add to our speech and that teachers have to help students develop an ear for the sounds within the words. One way to do this is through language play. Language play engages students in songs, nursery rhymes, poems, jingles, riddles, tongue twisters, good books, and other activities that are filled with words and phrases that emphasize the sound and rhythm of our language. Language learning occurs when teachers engage students in language play (Cunningham et al. 1998).

Jokes, riddles, and puns provide students with experiences that not only build language but also provide enjoyment and laughter. Tongue twisters allow students to play with words and enjoy the sounds of language. They also help with auditory and visual discrimination and physical articulation. In addition, tongue twisters are a natural way to involve students in alliteration. Nursery rhymes and poems bring home the connection between language, poetry, and music for children. Every nursery rhyme is full of rhythm, rhyme, and onomatopoeia. Songs are also filled with rhythm, rhyme, and alliteration, and almost all students love to sing. Another wonderful way to engage students in language play is through the use of children's literature. While reading books to students, teachers can focus on listening to the sounds in words.

A–Application

After reading the poem "The Giggling Gaggling Gaggle of Geese" (Prelutsky, 1983), the teacher writes the title on the board. The teacher and students play with the title, saying it several times as quickly as possible. They then brainstorm a list of animals—for example, dog, pig, rooster, horse, sheep. The teacher takes the first word and changes the title to "The Diggling Daggling Daggle of Dogs" and writes it on the board under the original title. The students try to say the new title quickly several times, listening to the sounds of the language. The students then get into four groups and are assigned one of the other animals from the list. The groups rewrite the title, using the first letter of their animal word, and then practice saying the title. After all groups have had time to practice their titles, each group comes to the front of the room, writes its new title on the board, and leads the class in repeating the title several times. The teacher then leads the class in "singing" the composition:

Giggling Gaggling Gaggle of Geese
Diggling Daggling Daggle of Dogs
Piggling Paggling Paggle of Pigs
Riggling Raggling Raggle of Roosters
Higgling Haggling Haggle of Horses
Shiggling Shaggling Shaggle of Sheep

D–Delivery

Language play consists of numerous ways to engage students in play-based oral language activities through songs, nursery rhymes, poems, jingles, riddles, tongue twisters, and good books. Each language-rich activity can be presented in its own way or a combination of ways. The key is simply surrounding students in activities filled with words and phrases that emphasize the sounds and rhythm of our language.

References

Cunningham, J., P. Cunningham, F. Hoffman, and H. Hopp. 1998. *Phonemic awareness and the teaching of reading.* A position statement from the Board of Directors of the International Reading Association. Newark, DE: International Reading Association.
Jongsma, K. 2000. Teaching—aids & devices—book review. *The Reading Teacher* 54 (1): 80–83.
Prelutsky, J. 1983. Zoo Doings; *Animal poems.* New York: HarperCollins.

PICTURE BINGO

When to Teach		Group Size		Grade Level	
Before Reading	📖	One-on-One		PreK–2	🏫
During Reading		Small Group	👥	3–5	
After Reading	📖	Whole Group	👥	6–8	

R–Rationale

BINGO is an interactive game format that can be used to heighten students' awareness of the sounds they hear in words. Phonemic awareness, as discussed earlier, is the ability to focus on and manipulate phonemes in spoken words (National Reading Panel 2000).

E–Explanation

The picture BINGO format requires students to view pictures on a BINGO card and then view a picture card shown by the caller. The student has to decide if the caller's picture card shares a common sound element with the pictures shown on the BINGO card.

A–Application

The example on the next page shows a BINGO card with words from nine different word families (i.e., -at, -ate, -ock, -est, -aw, -og, -an, -all, -in). Before actually beginning the game, the teacher should talk about each picture with students so that they are familiar with each one. Students should also understand and be able to recognize which pictures have similar sounds. In this particular game, because the focus is on common rimes, students should be listening for pictures that have the same ending. Once they are familiar with all of the picture cards, the caller starts the game by showing one of the pictures. Students have to identify the picture, then look at the pictures on their card, and find a match. For example, if the caller shows the picture of a nest, the students would have to recognize that the word that sounds similar to *nest* would be *pest*. This activity requires several layers of processing, since students have to view and identify the picture shown by the caller and then locate the picture on their BINGO card that has a similar sound. Play continues until someone has a BINGO, which could be three across, three down, or three diagonal.

Example of Picture BINGO Card

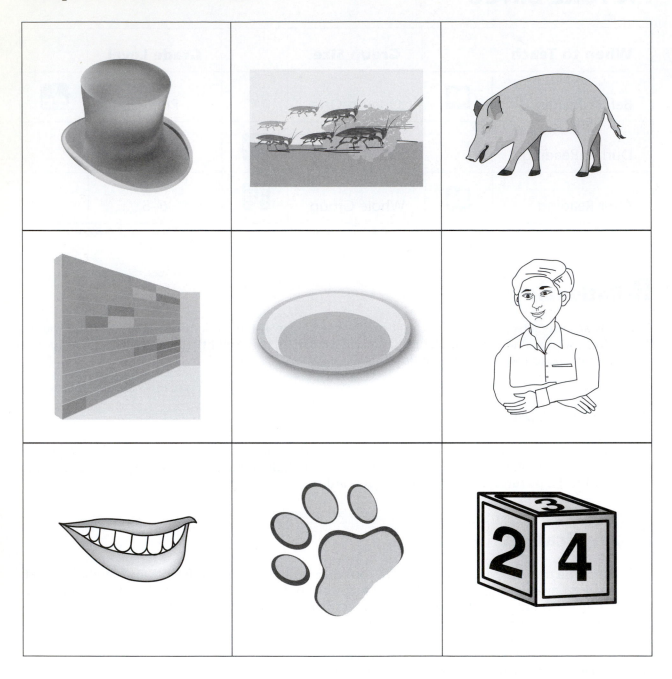

Call List

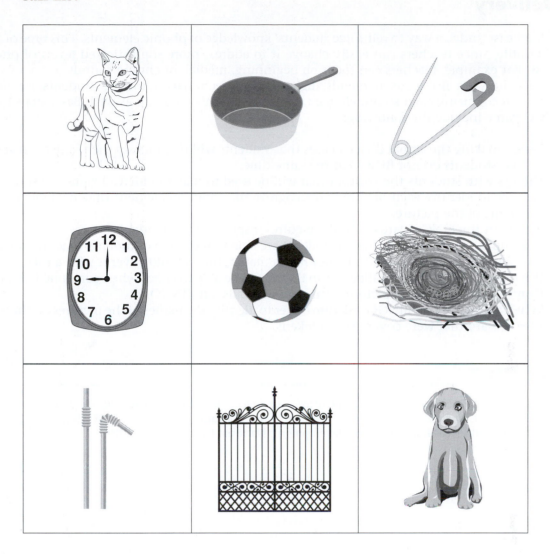

D–Delivery

BINGO is an easy and fun way to reinforce students' knowledge of phonic elements. This type of activity is also versatile, since teachers can easily change it to address more sophisticated levels of phonemic awareness. For example, teachers can focus on beginning, medial, or ending sounds or on a variety of all three. Teachers can also focus on blends, digraphs, or inflectional endings. As students become more proficient in recognizing each sound element, teachers can mix these up as well. Basic steps for using the BINGO game include the following:

1. When making the actual BINGO cards that students will use, mix up the pictures on each card so that students do not BINGO at the same time.
2. Discuss with students the pictures that will be used to play the BINGO game. Be sure students are able to identify each picture and recognize the common element they hear when they say the name of the picture.
3. Hand out the BINGO cards with the pictures displayed in individual squares.
4. Hold up a picture card so that all students are able to see it. Give students time to find a match on their picture BINGO cards. If they find a match, they should cover it with a token.
5. Place each picture that is called out to the side to be able to check when someone has a BINGO.
6. Continue showing each picture until someone calls out BINGO.
7. When a student does BINGO, ask him or her to identify the names of the pictures on the winning BINGO card that were covered with tokens.

Reference

National Reading Panel. 2000. *Teaching children to read: An evidence-based assessment of the scientific research literature on reading and its implications for reading instruction* (NIH Publication No. 00–4769). Washington, DC: National Institute of Child Health and Human Development, National Institutes of Health.

PICTURE SORTS

When to Teach		Group Size		Grade Level	
Before Reading	📖	One-on-One	👥	PreK–2	🏫
During Reading		Small Group	👥	3–5	
After Reading	📖	Whole Group	▦	6–8	

R–Rationale

Sorting is a powerful strategy students can use to make sense of words (Bear et al. 2004). This type of strategy is appropriate for emergent readers who do not have a large reading vocabulary. Students can sort pictures by initial sounds, consonant blends, digraphs, vowel sounds, or rhyming words.

E–Explanation

Picture sorts require students to view pictures and then make decisions about the sounds they hear in the words. This activity is usually begun with sorting for two sounds at a time (e.g., picture cards with the /b/ sound or /d/ sound). As students become more phonemically aware, teachers can have them begin to sort for medial sounds or ending sounds and can also increase the sorts to three or four sounds at a time. Sorting for medial or ending sounds requires students to segment the sounds in words and then identify which sound is the one in the middle or at the end. Given that understanding, it is best to use one-syllable words when doing picture sorts, because there are fewer sounds to confuse the students. This type of activity does not call for students to be able to tell that the /b/ sound is made with the letter *b*. Instead, students' skills in phonemic awareness are being reinforced as they recognize the sounds they hear in a word.

A–Application

One way to explore sounds is for students to sort picture cards according to a shared sound. For example, to sort for initial sounds, students can cut out the pictures and then group together the pictures that have the same beginning sounds. In the following picture sort activity, the groups would be these four:

- mouse, map, and man
- dice, deer, and duck
- tape, tub, and tent
- bat, barn, and ball

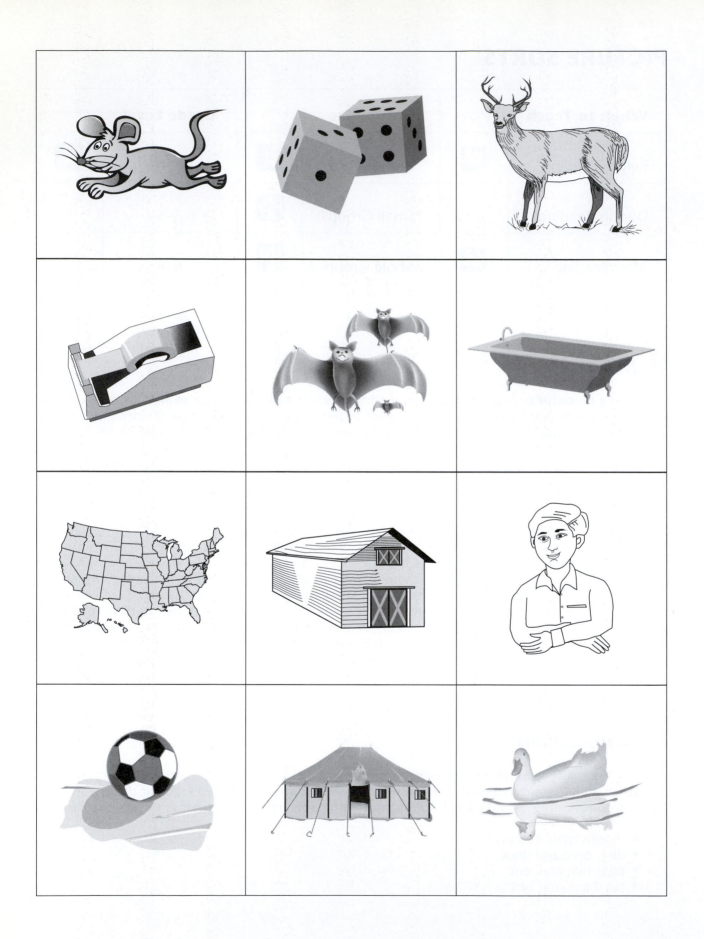

The teacher tells students that they are to sort the pictures to fit specific categories. Pictures of a top, dog, boy, and moon should appear at the tops of the four columns.

The teacher introduces the rest of the picture cards to students to make sure they recognize the pictures and they know the sound that is made at the beginning of each word. Students then sort the pictures and decide in which column to place each picture. After they finish sorting, the teacher asks them to read the pictures they have in each column and to identify why they placed each picture where they did. Students should be able to identify, for example, that the picture of the mouse was placed under the picture of the moon because they both start with the /m/ sound.

D–Delivery

Picture sorts can be used to reinforce students' awareness of sounds they hear in words. This type of activity requires students to identify the name of a picture and then determine what sound they hear at the beginning, middle, or ending of the word. Students then organize the pictures based on the common sounds that are shared.

1. Show students the pictures that will be used in the sorting activity to be sure they are familiar with the name of each picture. Hold up each card and ask students to identify what is in the picture.
2. Tell students that they will sort the words according to specific categories. Place the picture card for each category at the top of a column. There should be one column per sound being used in the sort. In addition, words that do not fit in any category can be included.
3. Ask students to sort the cards by placing each in a specific column.
4. Once they finish, have students read what they have in each column. Have them describe why they sorted the way they did by saying that the pictures of the bat and ball were placed under the "boy" column because they both start with the /b/ sound.

Reference

Bear, D. R., M. Invernizzi, S. Templeton, and F. Johnston. 2004. *Words their way: Word study for phonics, vocabulary, and spelling instruction.* 3rd ed. Upper Saddle River, NJ: Pearson.

Section III

Phonics

The English language is based on the alphabetic principle—the idea that letters represent sounds. To be proficient readers, students must understand the alphabetic principle (Adams 1990). Phonics is the relationship between the sounds in spoken words (i.e., phonology) and the spelling patterns in written words (i.e., orthography). When we help readers become knowledgeable about the alphabetic principle, we enable them to pronounce words they have never seen before.

More precisely, the idea behind the alphabetic principle is that there is a one-to-one correspondence between the phonemes, or sounds, and the graphemes, or letters, of words. Phonics involves understanding the relationship between phonemes and graphemes and the ways to use these relationships to read and write words. This all may seem like an easy concept where we simply teach students each phoneme/grapheme correspondence, and then they will be able to read. However, it is not that easy, because some English spellings are quite irregular.

Effective phonics instruction includes reading and writing words in both context and isolation. There is an ongoing discussion regarding how phonics should be taught to students. A major force driving this debate is the report of the National Reading Panel *Teaching Children to Read,* which emphasizes the need for systematic phonics instruction. Research cited in the report indicates that explicit and systematic phonics instruction is essential in students' reading progress and that knowledge of phonics is a strong predictor of successful reading (National Reading Panel 2000). Systematic phonics instruction, according to the report, is a way of teaching reading that emphasizes the acquisition of letter-sound correspondences and their use in reading and spelling words. There are several approaches that can be used in phonics instruction, such as synthetic phonics, analytic phonics, embedded phonics, analogy phonics, onset-rime phonics, and phonics through spelling. This section includes information on a few of these key approaches and then follows with other strategies that could be used to support this crucial skill area.

Researchers at the Center for the Improvement of Early Reading Achievement (CIERA) developed general guidelines based on the National Reading Panel report to assist teachers in evaluating whether a program is effective in phonics instruction. These guidelines state that effective programs offer phonics instruction that has the following characteristics (Armbruster, Lehr, and Osborn 2001, 16):

- It helps teachers explicitly and systematically instruct students in how to relate letters and sounds, how to break spoken words into sounds, and how to blend sounds to form words.
- It helps students understand why they are learning the relationships between letters and sounds.
- It helps students apply their knowledge of phonics as they read words, sentences, and text.
- It helps students apply what they learn about sounds and letters to their own writing.
- It can be adapted to the needs of individual students, based on assessment.
- It includes alphabetic knowledge, phonemic awareness, vocabulary development, and the reading of text, as well as systematic phonics instruction.

The goal of phonics instruction is to help students to learn and use the alphabetic principle. It is important that instruction is always placed within meaningful context, that there is systematic and explicit teaching of skills, and that students have continual opportunities to learn sound-symbol relations.

References

Adams, M. J. 1990. *Beginning to read: Thinking and learning about print*. Cambridge, MA: MIT Press.

Armbruster, B. B., F. Lehr, and J. Osborn. 2001. *Put reading first: The research building blocks for teaching children to read*. Jessup, MD: National Institute for Literacy.

National Reading Panel. 2000. *Teaching children to read: An evidence-based assessment of the scientific research literature on reading and its implications for reading instruction* (NIH Publication No. 00-4769). Washington, DC: National Institute of Child Health and Human Development, National Institutes of Health.

ANALYTIC PHONICS

When to Teach		Group Size		Grade Level	
Before Reading	📖	One-on-One	👥	PreK–2	🏫
During Reading		Small Group	👥	3–5	
After Reading	📖	Whole Group	👥	6–8	

R–Rationale

The National Reading Panel report defines analytic phonics instruction as teaching students how to analyze letter-sound relations in previously learned words in order to avoid pronouncing sounds in isolation (National Reading Panel 2000, 8). The purpose of analytic phonics is to introduce whole words to students and show them how to break the words into smaller, manageable parts.

E–Explanation

Analytic phonics teaches students specific phonic elements within the context of a whole word. The teacher presents the sound elements in the word *dog,* and the student must abstract the sound of each letter—/d/, /ŏ/, /g/—from the word. This approach avoids presenting sounds in isolation.

A–Application

The teacher introduces a group of words that share a common letter-sound relationship. For example, if the initial consonant /s/ is a focus, then the words could include *sail, sand, sat, sob,* and *see.* The teacher displays the words on cards or chart paper and points to each one as it is read aloud. Next, the teacher discusses with the students how the words look and sound alike or different. She says each word aloud slowly and asks students what sound they hear at the beginning of each word—/s/. Once this common-letter sound has been identified, the teacher discusses the words again. She says the words together and points to or underlines the letter *s* in each word. She asks the students what letter represents the sound of /s/ and forms a generalization about the sound that *s* makes (i.e., /s/). For example, the sound of the letter *s* is the sound we hear at the beginning of the word *sat.*

D–Delivery

Analytic phonics provides students with opportunities to analyze whole words and break them down into smaller, manageable parts.

1. Identify a list of words that share a common letter-sound relationship.
2. Say each word aloud to students and pause to let students repeat each word.

3. Ask students what they notice about the words, such as how the words look or sound alike or different.
4. Through this discussion, lead students into a recognition of the common letter-sound relationship.
5. Help students to identify a generalization about the letter-sound relationship.

Reference

National Reading Panel. 2000. *Teaching children to read: An evidence-based assessment of the scientific research literature on reading and its implications for reading instruction* (NIH Publication No. 00-4769). Washington, DC: National Institute of Child Health and Human Development, National Institutes of Health.

SYNTHETIC PHONICS

When to Teach		Group Size		Grade Level	
Before Reading	📖	One-on-One	👥	PreK–2	🏫
During Reading		Small Group	👥	3–5	
After Reading	📖	Whole Group	👥	6–8	

R–Rationale

The National Reading Panel report defines synthetic phonics as teaching students explicitly to convert letters into sounds and then blend the sounds to form recognizable words (National Reading Panel 2000, 8). The purpose of synthetic phonics is to first teach students specific graphemes, or letters, associated with a specific phoneme, or sound. Once students have learned the grapheme-phoneme relationships, they are able to use this knowledge to decode words.

E–Explanation

Synthetic phonics focuses on teaching the sounds that are represented by letters or combinations of letters; it teaches how to tie an individual letter to its corresponding sound. Students are asked to match the letter in words with the corresponding sound and then to form the word based on this process.

A–Application

The teacher introduces the letter *c* and teaches students the corresponding hard sound it can make: /k/. Next, he introduces the letter *a* and the sound this letter makes as a short vowel (i.e., /ă/) and then the letter *t* and the sound it makes: /t/. After these three sounds have been practiced, the teacher helps students blend them together to form the word *cat*.

D–Delivery

Synthetic phonics first teaches students letter-sound correspondence; then students practice blending the sounds together to make words.

1. Introduce each letter name to students.
2. Teach the sound that each letter makes.
3. As each letter is written on the board or chart paper, point to the letter, and say the sound that each letter makes.

4. Make a hand motion to indicate blending the sounds together.
5. Continue this process until students can easily recognize the letter and the corresponding sound.

Reference

National Reading Panel. 2000. *Teaching children to read: an evidence-based assessment of the scientific research literature on reading and its implications for reading instruction* (NIH Publication No. 00-4769). Washington, DC: National Institute of Child Health and Human Development, National Institutes of Health.

EMBEDDED PHONICS

When to Teach		Group Size		Grade Level	
Before Reading	📖	One-on-One	👥	PreK–2	🏫
During Reading	📖	Small Group	👥	3–5	🏫
After Reading	📖	Whole Group	👥	6–8	

R–Rationale

Also known as phonics in context, the embedded phonics approach encourages learners to use letter-sound clues along with context to identify words encountered in text. The National Reading Panel (2000) reports that embedded phonics approaches have been used as part of explicit and systematic phonics instruction. This type of approach is often more effective when combined with other types of approaches, such as synthetic or analytic phonics instruction.

E–Explanation

Embedded phonics instruction can be easily built into shared reading, guided reading, and other reading experiences. During a shared reading of Nancy Shaw's *Sheep in a Jeep*, for example, teachers can draw attention to the rime *–eep* found in *sheep* and *jeep*. Other examples include Dr. Seuss's *One Fish, Two Fish, Red Fish, Blue Fish*, which features the /ĭ/ sound along with the phonogram *–ish*, or the /ă/ sound in Dr. Seuss's *Cat in the Hat*, along with the phonogram *–at*. As the book is read, the teacher can pause at strategic places with phonic elements that can be emphasized. At the end of the story, the teacher can ask students to brainstorm words that fit a specific phonic skill or can reread the book and have students signal when they hear a word with a particular sound (e. g., /ă/). The teacher should write each identified word on chart paper or the chalkboard, also breaking down the other sounds that are heard in the word (e. g., *hat*—/h/ /ă/ /t/). With students who have been working on recognizing the sound symbol correspondence, the teacher can ask their help in identifying the actual letter that corresponds to the sound (e. g., /h/ = h).

A–Application

For kindergarten students, the teacher reads aloud the nursery rhyme "Hickory, Dickory, Dock." For first graders, the teacher displays the nursery rhyme on chart paper or through a projection system. The teacher reads the rhyme aloud to students while they listen, or she points to the words on the chart paper to track the print. The teacher emphasizes the rhythmic pattern of the text as it is read. Once students become familiar with the nursery rhyme, the teacher encourages them to join in with the reading. As the story is read, the teacher can also add clapping or snapping to go along with the rhythm of the nursery rhyme.

The teacher repeats this several times and then reads the rhyme once again, asking students to listen for any words that sound like the word *dock*.

Hickory, Dickory, Dock,
The mouse ran up the clock.
The clock struck one,
The mouse ran down.
Hickory, Dickory, Dock.

The answer, of course, is *clock*. The teacher talks with students about what it is that makes these words sound the same—the ending *ock*. She can also talk to them about common sounds that are heard, such as the /ŏ/ sound made by the letter *o* and the /k/ sound made by the letters *ck*. Next, the teacher asks students to listen for any words that sound like *hickory*. The answer is *dickory*. The teacher says the words *hickory* and *dickory* slowly and asks the students what part of the words sound alike—the ending. The teacher can talk about numerous sounds here: the /ĭ/ sound, the /k/ sound, the /er/ sound made by the letters *or*, and the /ē/ sound made by the letter *y*.

D–Delivery

The major goal of embedded phonics instruction is to teach students to use letter-sound clues along with context clues to help them decode words in a text. The reading of a text, combined with a discussion afterwards, helps to reinforce these connections more explicitly for students.

1. Select a text that includes phonic elements to be targeted.
2. Prior to reading the story with the class, make a list of the words that fit each phonic element, or use removable notes to mark places in the text to stop and emphasize a particular phonic element.
3. Prior to reading the story, access students' prior knowledge, and build background knowledge as needed for the topic or concept of the book. Tell students that this book contains either some phonic sounds that the class has worked on previously or new ones they will be learning. Tell students each sound to listen for during the reading of the story.
4. Read the book aloud to students, using a shared reading format while they listen.
5. Reread the book again, but this time ask students to help figure out words by using letter-sound and context clues.
6. After the reading, make a written list of the words that were discussed in the story. If possible, organize the words according to shared sounds (e. g., the /ē/ sound in *sheep* and *jeep* in *Sheep in a Jeep*).
7. As an extension of this activity, ask students to work with a partner to write each word on a card and then to sort the words according to shared sounds.

Reference

National Reading Panel. 2000. *Teaching children to read: An evidence-based assessment of the scientific research literature on reading and its implications for reading instruction.* Washington, DC: National Institute for Child Health and Human Development, National Institutes of Health.

ANALOGY PHONICS

When to Teach		Group Size		Grade Level	
Before Reading		One-on-One		PreK–2	
During Reading		Small Group		3–5	
After Reading		Whole Group		6–8	

R–Rationale

In the analogy approach, also called the analogic approach, students use their knowledge of patterns in known words to identify unfamiliar words. For example, if students are familiar with the word family –ill, they can successfully read words such as *bill, dill, fill, gill, hill,* and so forth. Teaching by analogy is another phonics approach that is discussed in the National Reading Panel report (2000, 2–89). As with any program, its success depends on the use of a planned, sequential set of phonic elements, which should be taught explicitly and systematically.

E–Explanation

When we teach students to use analogy to decode and spell words, we involve them in recognizing how the spelling of an unfamiliar word is similar to that of a word already known. In order to do this, the reader must first access the known word and then apply that knowledge to a new word. For example, if I know how to spell *set*, then I can spell *met, let, bet,* and *get*. Teaching by analogy draws on students' knowledge of word families. It also reinforces students' awareness of onset (i.e., the part of the syllable prior to the vowel) and rime (i.e., the vowel and the rest of the syllable). In the word *pot,* the onset would be *p-* and the rime would be *-ot*. If students are able to break a syllable into onset and rime, that helps them recognize a common part that is shared by words, such as the *-ot* family in *pot, cot, got, hot,* and *lot*.

This type of approach is also found in spelling programs for older students (e. g., in Grades 4–8), for whom the focus is on derivational relations, such as Greek and Latin roots or other parts of words. The idea behind derivational relations is to help students recognize specific parts of words (e. g., *tele-*) and know that if they can spell *telescope,* they are closer to spelling *telegraph, telephone, television,* and *telecast*. This type of program goes a step further to make a vocabulary connection, teaching students to determine the meaning based on their knowledge that *tele-* means "far off" or "at a distance."

A–Application

The analogy approach can be used to build on the concept of onset and rime to heighten students' awareness about common parts shared by words. For example, the teacher introduces the rime *-at* and then tells students the word *rat*. He asks students if they can hear the *-at* in *rat*. They all work together to brainstorm other words that could go with the rime *-at,* such as *bat, cat, fat, hat, mat, pat,* and *sat.* The teacher lists these words on chart paper to display in the room. As each word is written, he breaks down the sounds in the word by onset and rime and then asks students to help spell each part. The teacher writes each letter to reinforce these sound-symbol relationships. After the word is written, he asks students to say it aloud again while he points to the onset and rime. Then he blends the sounds together to say the whole word. This chart paper then becomes a resource for students when they are trying to see how a word is spelled.

Another example of this analogy approach is shown in the photo. The teacher had already worked with the students as a group; then the students worked independently in centers, where they used magnetic letters to spell words.

Carrice Cummins

On this particular day, the teacher was helping this child with the idea that if she can spell the word *night,* she can also spell *fight.* The child followed the spelling of these two words with the spelling of the word *right.*

D–Delivery

The analogy approach instructs students on how to use their knowledge of patterns in known words to identify unfamiliar words.

1. Select a word family to focus on, and then identify five to eight words that use this word family. It is best to use one-syllable words with beginning readers and writers, because it is easier for them to break the word apart into the onset and rime.
2. Tell students they will be learning how to spell words that all belong to the same word family, because the words share the same ending. Write the word family on chart paper, the overhead, or another projection system.
3. Introduce the words to students one at a time. Say the word aloud to them, and ask them to repeat the word.
4. Then repeat the word again and break it down into onset and rime. Ask students to repeat the onset and rime.
5. Next, ask students what sound(s) they hear in the onset. Work with them to identify the letter that corresponds to that sound. Write each part of the onset and rime as it is identified.
6. Repeat this process with each word. Once all the words have been added to the list, ask students to say again what these words have in common.

7. In an extension to the activity, give students clues and then ask them to point to the word on the list that relates to that clue. For example, if the clue is "This animal likes to eat cheese," the word is *rat*.
8. Brainstorm together some other words that can be formed using the phonogram. As each new word is identified, add it to the list of words on the chart paper.

Reference

National Reading Panel. 2000. *Teaching children to read: An evidence-based assessment of the scientific research literature on reading and its implications for reading instruction.* Washington, DC: National Institute for Child Health and Human Development, National Institutes of Health.

BINGO

When to Teach		Group Size		Grade Level	
Before Reading	📖	One-on-One		PreK–2	🏫
During Reading		Small Group	👥	3–5	
After Reading	📖	Whole Group	👥	6–8	

R–Rationale

BINGO is an interactive game format that provides students with another opportunity to make connections between phonic elements they hear in words and the written symbols that represent those sounds. This strategy differs from picture BINGO, since students are required to make the connection between the sound and the symbol. This strategy is another form of word study, which gives students time to explore what they know about letter-sound correspondence. The major purpose of word study is to help students "examine words in order to reveal consistencies within the written language system and to help students master the recognition, spelling, and meaning of specific words" (Bear et al. 2004, 4).

E–Explanation

Phonics BINGO is used to reinforce phonic elements students are learning. Instead of the traditional B-12, teachers call out a word, and students have to determine what phonic element it includes and then mark it on their BINGO cards. For example, teachers could organize a BINGO game with words containing different types of digraphs, such as *ch*, *th*, or *sh*. The actual BINGO card would show different digraphs scattered around the card, and the teacher would call out words that have those sounds, such as *chip* (*ch*), *fish* (*sh*), or *thumb* (*th*). When the word *chip* is called out, students would mark a space on their card that has the *ch* printed.

A–Application

This example shows a BINGO card that includes short and long vowel sounds. Students are listening to words with short or long vowel sounds and then deciding which word on the BINGO card also has that sound. This requires several layers of processing, since students have to listen to the word, segment the word and identify the vowel sound, and then match the sound to another word on the card that has that same vowel sound. Examples of words teachers could use on the call list include these: *cob*, *bet*, *feet*, *soap*, *sick*, *rate*, *rug*, *bat*.

BINGO		
hot	hit	egg
nice	seat	make
rope	cap	cup

To play the game, the teacher calls out a word, such as *cob*, and students have to recognize that the vowel sound is /ŏ/ and then place their marker on the word *hot*. The teacher repeats this process until someone has a BINGO. Again, the words on the BINGO cards should be shuffled around to make different versions of the card; otherwise, everyone will BINGO!

D–Delivery

BINGO is an easy and fun way to reinforce students' knowledge of phonic elements. This type of activity is also versatile; teachers can easily change it to address more sophisticated levels of phonic awareness. For example, teachers can focus on beginning, medial, or ending sounds or on a variety of all three. Teachers can also focus on blends, digraphs, and/or inflectional endings. The basic steps for this BINGO game are:

1. Give students the BINGO cards with the words written on them, or give everyone a blank BINGO card and tell students to write down one word in each square of the BINGO card as the words are called out.
2. Keep a master list of these words, along with the words that will be used from the call list. The words to be called out can be written on index cards to use during the game.
3. Call out the words. After saying each word, break it down into the sounds students hear (i.e., *pot*—/p/ /ŏ/ /t/). This helps students identify the targeted sound.
4. Have students place pieces of paper or other markers on their cards as each word is called out.
5. The winner is the first to cover a row of words across, down, or on the diagonal.

Reference

Bear, D. R., M. Invernizzi, S. Templeton, and F. Johnston. 2004. *Words their way: Word study for phonics, vocabulary, and spelling instruction*. 3rd ed. Upper Saddle River, NJ: Pearson.

CLOZE

When to Teach		Group Size		Grade Level	
Before Reading		One-on-One		PreK–2	
During Reading		Small Group		3–5	
After Reading		Whole Group		6–8	

R–Rationale

The technical definition of a cloze activity is one that deletes every *n*th word (e. g., the fifth or seventh) from a segment of text. A cloze activity can be used as a general way of reinforcing word recognition along with comprehension by targeting specific phonic elements in words. It can also be used to focus on sight words or words used for vocabulary instruction. Teachers can model for students how to identify missing words: drawing on prior knowledge, constructing meaning as the text is read, and analyzing letter clues in the missing words. Readers develop a powerful tool for word identification when they combine meaning clues with phonic clues (Vacca et al. 2006).

E–Explanation

When developing a cloze passage, teachers should leave in the first and last sentences and usually all proper nouns. Cloze is commonly used in assessments to see how students respond to words that are missing and to determine what reading strategies they use to identify missing words. We use the cloze activity as a way to select words in a passage that contain specific phonic elements. Parts of the words are deleted, but students are left with a few letter clues to draw on when they read the text. This type of strategy encourages the use of cross-checking, since students are using context clues along with letter clues.

A–Application

In a cloze activity that reinforces use of context along with graphophonic elements (i.e., letter-sound), the teacher leaves some parts of the words visible to draw students' attention to these clues. In the first example, students would use the letter clue *h* along with the context clues of bunny and forest to determine that the missing word is *hopped*. If students come up with more than one option for the word, (for example, hops) the teacher reveals another letter and asks students which of the words that were discussed no longer fit the blank.

The little bunny h▭ through the forest.

Teachers use segments of familiar text from nursery rhymes, favorite poems, or stories the class has been reading. For example, with the nursery rhyme "Jack and Jill," the teacher leaves blank parts of words that relate to phonic elements the class has been studying:

> Jack and Jill ran up the h_____
> To fetch a pail of water.
> Jack f_____ down and broke his crown,
> And J_____ came tumbling after.

The word part omitted were taken from the common word families –ill and –ell. The teacher first reads the nursery rhyme with the words in place to help students become familiar with the words in the text. She reads it several times, encouraging students to join in during the reading. The teacher tracks the text by pointing to each word as it is read to draw students' attention to the words. After this has been done several times, the teacher asks students to cover their eyes while she covers up parts of the words. She then reads the story again and lets students fill in each missing word. She asks them which word is missing as she displays three words on cards below the nursery rhyme—*Jill, hill,* and *fell*. The teacher asks students if they know which word goes in each blank in the nursery rhyme. They read the words together and try each word in each blank to see which one makes sense.

D–Delivery

A cloze activity shows students how to use both context and graphophonic clues to identify unfamiliar words they encounter in a text.

1. Select a short segment of text or specific sentences from a story, poem, or other source.
2. Read the passage aloud to students as a read-aloud or as a shared reading activity. You can also skip this step and go straight to the passage with selected parts of words covered up.
3. Cover up parts of selected words that include a targeted phonic element. Do not cover up too many words in the passage; it is difficult to construct meaning when too much of the text is missing. If a big book is being used, sticky notes work well. You can also use sticky notes to cover up material that is shown on the overhead. If a computer and projection system are being used, you can use text boxes in the program to cover up word parts.
4. Read the first sentence with students, using the word *blank* to indicate the missing word.
5. Talk with students about the clues they can use to help identify the missing word (i.e., context clues and letter clues).
6. Ask students what word would make sense in the blank. Be sure to reinforce whether the words students suggest also match up with the letter clues that are showing.
7. Once the class has reached a consensus about the word, read the sentence with that word inserted. Ask whether the sentence makes sense.
8. Repeat this process with other missing words in the text.

Reference

Vacca, J. L., R. T. Vacca, M. K. Gove, L. C. Burkey, L. A. Lenhart, and C. A. McKeon. 2006. *Reading and learning to read*. 6th ed. Boston: Pearson.

ONSET AND RIME FLIP BOOKS

When to Teach		Group Size		Grade Level	
Before Reading	📖	One-on-One	👥	PreK–2	🏫
During Reading		Small Group	👥	3–5	
After Reading	📖	Whole Group		6–8	

R–Rationale

Onset and rime flip books are made of strips of paper that allow various onsets to be added to a rime. This type of strategy provides more explicit instruction and reinforcement with word families. Students also begin to see how these patterns are found in other words, such as words ending in *–it, -at, -in-, -an,* and *–all,* and they use this knowledge of similar patterns to read by analogy (Ehri and McCormick 2004).

E–Explanation

The onset and rime flip book is a way to let students practice words from the same word family. It provides one more approach students can use when they are trying to decode words in other contexts. Students are able to see that they know a chunk, or part, of a word, and they learn to make new words by simply adding extra letters to the beginning. This strategy begins to move students beyond sounding out a word in a letter-by-letter manner. More efficient readers recognize parts of words more quickly, and they apply this skill when working with texts.

A–Application

The teacher makes an onset and rime flip book by first writing the rime, such as *–ill,* on a word card, leaving a blank space for the changing onset.

The teacher punches a hole in the upper left corner of the card so that the different onsets can be added to the rime, using a metal ring. Each onset is written on a smaller card, also hole-punched, so that it can be flipped on top of the longer strip that displays the rime. For example, the onsets *b-, d-, f-, h-, k-, m-, p-, s-, st-, t-,* and *w-* can be flipped onto *–ill* to make *bill, dill, fill, hill, kill, mill, pill, sill, still, till,* and *will.*

Students can make a new word simply by turning over another small card.

Students continue to flip the pages of the book to make the rest of the words found in the *–ill* family.

D–Delivery

The onset and rime flip book reinforces students' awareness of how different onsets can be added to a rime to form new words.

1. Cut tagboard or construction paper into strips that are about 2 inches in width and 6 to 7 inches in length.
2. Leave one of the strips long (2″ × 7″). Cut the other strips in half.
3. Write the rime on the long strip of paper, toward the right-hand side. Be sure to leave room for the smaller strips to flip over to form words; without enough room, students have difficulty reading the new words. In the example that follows, the onsets range from one letter (e.g., *c-*) to three letters (e.g., *spl-*).

4. Write each onset on a smaller strip. These are examples of possible onsets.

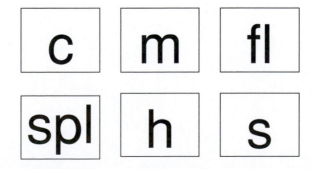

5. Punch a hole in the upper left corner of the long strip as well as the short strips.

6. Stack the short strips on top of the long strip, and thread the metal ring through all the holes to keep the cards together. You can reinforce the holes with reinforcement labels that are available in any office supply store.
7. Let students enjoy the onset and rime flip books.

Reference

Ehri, L. C., and S. McCormick. 2004. Phases of word learning: Implications for instruction with delayed and disabled readers. *Theoretical models and processes of teaching* (5th ed.), ed. R. B. Ruddell and N. J. Unrau, 365–89. Newark, DE: International Reading Association.

MAKING WORDS

When to Teach		Group Size		Grade Level	
Before Reading		One-on-One		PreK–2	🏫
During Reading		Small Group	👥	3–5	🏫
After Reading	📖	Whole Group	👥	6–8	🏫

R–Rationale

Making words is a manipulative activity in which students learn how to look for patterns in words and then how to change letters in words to make new words (Cunningham 2005). The strategy helps make more concrete the abstract concept of how words work. Making words helps students develop phonemic awareness as they stretch out words and listen for the sounds; it also helps them learn important information about phonics and spelling.

E–Explanation

Making words is a fun strategy that gives students letters to use in building words. The activity can be used as soon as children have a basic understanding of the relationship between sounds and letters. The individual letters can be written on index cards or can be purchased magnetic letters. The teacher guides students through this process by providing letters, letter patterns, and context clues that students use to determine a specific word that can be formed using the given letters. As students manipulate the letters, they learn how changing just one letter or moving the letters around can result in a brand new word. A lesson on making words usually takes about fifteen to twenty minutes to complete, with the majority of the time being devoted to making the words and the remaining time spent doing sorting activities and application.

A–Application

The teacher and a small group of first-grade students sit around a table. The teacher gives each student a baggie with the letters for the lesson: *e, i, s, d, p, r.* Students are also given individual pocket charts in which to place their letters as they are using them. The teacher has the students pull out the letters as he reminds them which are vowels and which are consonants. The students separate the letters into two categories: vowels and consonants.

The teacher explains that the students are going to first make a two-letter word using the letters. The teacher gives the students a clue: "The word rhymes with *his.*" The students use two letter cards to form the word *is.* The teacher also has a large pocket chart and letters so he can model for students who have trouble. The teacher and students then say the word together, spell the word together, and repeat the word again.

Students return their letters to the vowel and consonant categories, and the process continues, next making three-letter words. The teacher uses the following clues to guide the students in making their words:

1. "This three-letter word means the same thing as taking a drink of water." (*sip*)
2. "Change one letter in *sip* to make this new word, which means to tear something." (*rip*)
3. "Change the first letter in this word to make the word that means to go for a swim in the water." (*dip*)
4. "Use three different letters to make the color of a stop sign." (*red*)
5. "Make the word that would complete this sentence: 'I told my dad, "Yes, _____ , I will do that right now."'" (*sir*)

The teacher then guides the students in making four-letter words, using the following clues:

1. "This word would fill in the blank in this sentence: 'I will go for a _____ in the car.'" (*ride*)
2. "Change one letter in this word to make a new word that rhymes with *ride*." (*side*)
3. "This word means when a fruit is ready to eat." (*ripe*)

The teacher then shifts the students into making five-letter words, using the following clues:

1. "Make a word that describes what happens when the bathroom faucet leaks—it does what?" (*drips*)
2. "This next word means something you feel when you know you have done a good job. You have a lot of _____ in a job well done." (*pride*)

The teacher then guides the students in using all of the letters to form the word that describes this bug (*spider*):

1. "It comes in a lot of shapes and sizes."
2. "Some of the names of this type of bug are black widow and tarantula."
3. "It has eight legs."
4. "It can spin a web that traps the food it will eat."

If students have difficulty spelling the word, the teacher can provide additional clues, such as that it starts with these two letters—*sp*, it ends with the /er/ sound, and/or the middle sound is the same as the middle sound of the word *riding*. Finally, the teacher has the students say the word aloud and spell it together.

The teacher then guides the students in sorting activities. Using the words formed in the previous activities, the teacher and students look for patterns in the words. Together they come up with the following categories:

Short vowel sounds—*sip, rip*
Long vowel sounds—*side, ride, ripe, pride*
Rhyming words—*sip, rip, dip*

To conclude the lesson, the teacher takes magnetic letters and makes the word *ride* (made earlier in the lesson). He distributes the following magnetic letters to each student in the group: *s, t, h, w*. One at a time the students change the *r* with their letters, making a new word each time. The teacher explains to the students that if they encounter a word they do not know in their reading, like *tide*, they can remember the word they *do* know, like *ride*, and mentally change the beginning sound just like they did with the magnetic letters.

D–Delivery

Lessons on making words generally have three steps: making words, looking for patterns by sorting words, and transferring new knowledge to reading application.

Making Words

1. Decide what the "big word" is that can be made with all the letters. In choosing this word, consider books the children are reading and the letter-sound patterns you can draw their attention to through the sorting at the end.
2. Make a list of other words you can make from these letters.
3. Pick 12 to 15 of these words using these criteria:
   a. Words that have the pattern you want to emphasize.
   b. Little words and big words so that the lesson is multilevel. (Making the little words helps your slowest students; making the big words challenges your most accelerated students).
   c. Words that can be made with the same letters in different places (*cold/clod*) so that children are reminded that the ordering of letters is crucial.
   d. A proper name or two to remind students that names need capital letters.
   e. Words that most students have in their listening vocabularies.
4. Write all the words on index card, and order them from smallest to biggest.
5. On the back of each index card, write clues you can use in helping the students make their words.
6. Once you have the two-letter, three-letter, etc. words together, order them so you can emphasize letter patterns and the effect of changing the position of letters or of changing or adding just one letter.
7. Distribute letter cards to the students, but keep a set of cards to use for modeling.
8. Make words—moving from two-letter words to longer words and finally using all of the letters to make the original big word.

Sorting Words

1. Read aloud with the students all of the words made in the lesson.
2. Have the students sort the words, looking for patterns. Students can sort for certain types of phonograms, spelling patterns, endings, prefixes, suffixes, rhyming words, compound words, and homophones.

Transferring Words

Select one word from the making words phase of the lesson, and help students see how knowledge of one word can help to decode or spell other words.

Reference

Cunningham, P. M. 2005. *Phonics they use: Words for reading and writing.* 4th ed. New York: HarperCollins.

RAINBOW ALPHABET ARC

When to Teach		Group Size		Grade Level	
Before Reading		One-on-One	👥	PreK–2	🏫
During Reading		Small Group	👥	3–5	
After Reading	📖	Whole Group	👥	6–8	

R–Rationale

The rainbow alphabet arc is a strategy designed to provide students with hands-on manipulatives to use in making words. It is a form of making words (Cunningham 2005) and is especially beneficial in helping students see the role that vowels play in words.

E–Explanation

The rainbow alphabet arc provides students with manipulatives to use in practicing their understanding of making words. It is especially helpful when studying vowel patterns, because students can see that vowel placement in a word controls the sound of the vowel. The rainbow alphabet can be made from a variety of materials, but poker chips with white stick-on dots seem to work best. Consonants are white chips, vowels are red chips and consonant digraphs are blue chips. You will need two each for *e, w,* and *y.* Use one red chip and one white chip for the letters *w* and *y* as they can serve as both a vowel and a consonant. The two vowels (red chips) allow students to make words containing double ee (i.e., feet, week). The letters should be written with a black marker on the white dots in the center of each chip. Some teachers write capital letters on one side of the chip and lower-case letters on the other side.

The chips can be placed in pint-size baggies and distributed to each student before the lesson. Students place their chips on the table in front of them in an arc shape. The easiest way to have students make their arc is to have them place the letter *a* on the lower left edge of their working space, the letter *z* at the lower right edge of their working space, and the letters *m* and *n* at the top middle of their working space. They then fill in the spaces with the letters in alphabetical order, making a rainbow shape. The strategy works extremely well when teaching vowel patterns but can also be used just as a making words activity in which students change out letters to form new words.

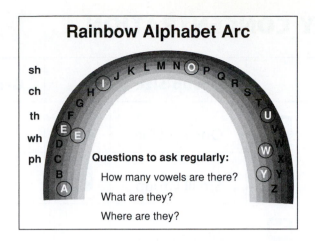

Rainbow Alphabet Arc

sh
ch
th
wh
ph

A B C D E E F G H I J K L M N O P Q R S T U V W X Y Y Z

Questions to ask regularly:

How many vowels are there?

What are they?

Where are they?

A–Application

First-grade students have been studying short vowel sounds and the rule that one vowel in the middle of two consonants usually has a short sound. To provide practice in seeing the rule in action, the teacher decides to use the rainbow alphabet arc strategy. She puts the students in pairs and passes out the rainbow-letter baggies. The students use their letters to make their rainbow arcs. The teacher reminds the students of the vowel rule they have been studying. She then directs the students to pull down the letter *c* into the large open space under their arcs. Next, she has them pull down the letter *t* and the letter *t*. The teacher asks the students, "How many vowels are in the word?" and the students answer, "One." She then asks, "What is it?" and the students reply, "*a*." She asks, "Where is the vowel *a*?" and they answer, "In the middle." The teacher reminds the students that when a vowel is squished in the middle between two consonants, it usually says its short sound. She and the students sound out the word together—/k/ /ă/ /t/, cat. The students then return their letters to the arc.

The teacher continues calling out one-syllable, short-vowel words and directing the students to pull down the appropriate letters (as students mature in their understanding, they can pull down the letters without the teacher's direct guidance). Each time before the students decode the word, the teacher reminds them of the vowel rule by asking these questions:

How many vowels are in the word?
What is it?
Where is it?

D–Delivery

The rainbow arc provides a concrete way for students to see how letters and sounds go together to form words.

1. Develop sets of letters for each student or small group of students.
2. Have students place their letter chips alphabetically on their desks in an arc format to resemble a rainbow.
3. Call out a word, and have the students pull chips from the arc to form the word. These words can be related to a specific vowel pattern or skill being taught, or the activity can just be practice forming words in general.
4. As words are formed, remind the students of the rule or pattern they are studying.
5. Have students return their chips to the arc for the next word.

Reference

Cunningham, P. M. 2005. *Phonics they use: Words for reading and writing.* 4th ed. New York: HarperCollins.

WORD FAMILY CONCENTRATION

When to Teach		Group Size		Grade Level	
Before Reading		One-on-One		PreK–2	
During Reading		Small Group		3–5	
After Reading		Whole Group		6–8	

R–Rationale

Word family concentration is an interactive game format that focuses on common word families to draw students' attention to larger parts, or chunks, of words. Students become aware of how a variety of onsets can be added to a rime to make many new words.

E–Explanation

In a study of word families, there is no particular order that has been identified as the best. However, Bear et al. (2004) recommends beginning with word families that have the short *a* (e.g., *–at, -an, -ad, -ap, -ack*), because these patterns can be found in early reading materials. For word family concentration, the teacher selects pairs of words to use in the game; each pair should share a particular word family (e.g., *sell, bell; bat, hat*). When using this game for the first time with young students, the teacher should have previously talked about the words the students will see on each card. In addition, the word families that are included in the game should have been discussed. The teacher could even have done a class sorting activity with the words to reinforce the rime that each word pair shares. Beginning consonants can be added to 38 phonograms to make 654 different one-syllable words move (Fry 1998, 620–22). Examples follow:

Examples of Common Phonograms

Rime	Example Words
-ab	cab, jab, crab
-ack	sack, rack, track
-ag	bag, wag, sag
-ail	pail, nail, tail
-ain	pain, chain, plain
-ake	cake, take, brake
-am	ham, jam, ram
-an	pan, ran, man
-ank	tank, blank, drank
-ap	cap, clap, trap
-at	cat, fat, bat

-ay	jay, day, play
-ed	red, fed, led
-eed	feed, need, freed
-ell	bell, tell, yell
-est	nest, reset, test
-ew	new, grew, blew
-ick	sick, quick, chick
-ight	light, right, night
-ill	hill, fill, spill
-im	swim, him, brim
-in	pin, win, thin
-ine	line, nine, shine
-ing	ring, sing, thing
-ink	pink, rink, drink
-ip	tip, skip, trip
-ob	cob, job, rob
-ock	sock, rock, lock
-op	mop, top, hop
-ore	more, tore, score
-ot	pot, not, got
-out	pout, trout, spout
-ow	low, slow, snow
-uck	luck, truck, buck
-ug	rug, bug, tug
-um	gum, bum, plum
-unk	sunk, junk, skunk
-y	my, dry, try

A–Application

The teacher focuses on the word families *–ight* and *–ine* in this word family concentration game. He uses these words for the word family *–ight—knight, light, right, fight*—and these words for the word family *–ine—line, nine, pine, shine*. The teacher writes each word on a separate index card, introduces the words to the students, and talks about the rime that is shared by some of the words. For example, the teacher asks students to identify what the words *pine* and *line* have in common. Then he does this with other word pairs, such as *knight* and *light*. The students should be able to recognize the words that sound alike and share a rime. Once the teacher is sure that the students can read the words, the index cards are placed face down on a flat surface.

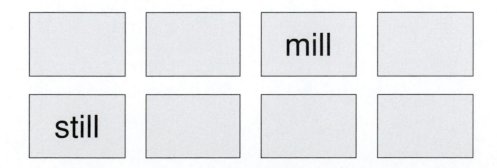

Students then take turns turning over two cards at a time, reading the word that is on each card, and deciding if the words share a rime. If they do, the student keeps the two word cards. If there is no match, the cards are turned back over, and the next person has a turn. An important part of the game is that the student pronounces each word aloud. It is not enough to visually recognize that the words share a rime; students should actually read the words aloud and confirm that the words do or do not match. Students repeat this process until all the words have been paired together. In this particular situation, there are only two rimes. The difficulty level of this strategy can easily be varied by adding more pairs as well as different word families.

D–Delivery

Word family concentration is an interactive way to reinforce students' awareness of larger parts of words.

1. Select word families to include in the word family concentration game. Write each word on a separate index card.
2. Introduce the words to students, and talk about the rime that is shared by some of the words. Remember to ask students to identify what the words have in common.
3. Next, place the index cards face down on a flat surface. Have students take turns turning over two cards at a time, reading the word that is on each card, and deciding if the words share a rime. If they do, the student keeps the two word cards. If there is no match, the cards are turned back over, and the next person has a turn.
4. Be sure that the students pronounce all the words aloud as they turn over the word cards.
5. Have students repeat this process until all the words have been paired together.

References

Bear, D. R., M. Internizzi, S. Templeton, F. Johnston. 2004. *Words their way: Word study for phonics, vocabulary, and spelling instruction.* (3rd ed.). Upper Saddle River, NJ: Pearson.
Fry, E. 1998. The most common phonograms. *The Reading Teacher* 51: 620–22.

WORD WALL

When to Teach		Group Size		Grade Level	
Before Reading		One-on-One		PreK–2	
During Reading		Small Group		3–5	
After Reading		Whole Group		6–8	

R–Rationale

A word wall is an alphabetical arrangement of words that students have been learning and that are displayed on the classroom wall. Word walls are an effective way of promoting the use of word study in the classroom (Cunningham 2005; Gunning 2008). The words placed on a word wall can be high frequency words, words from a particular story students are reading, or even words from a unit of study in a content area. The intent is to choose words that the students can use often in their reading and writing. By displaying these words on a word wall and having conversations about the words, teachers provide students with a visual resource that can help scaffold their use of these words in other contexts.

E–Explanation

A word wall is started at the beginning of the school year with four to five words added each week. The words are placed alphabetically on a portion of the classroom wall or bulletin board. Some basic characteristics of a word wall include (Brabham and Villaume 2001):

1. It is a developmentally appropriate collection of words.
2. Words are selected for specific instructional purposes.
3. Familiar words remain on the wall as needed, while new words are added each week.
4. The words displayed on the wall assist students in independent reading and writing.
5. A word wall serves as a conversational scaffold that structures the way students study, think about, and use words.

A word wall should be more than just words displayed on a wall. The teacher should work with the students on a daily basis to study and talk about the words, so that the words become an integral part of their literacy activities. The more aware students are of the words shown on the wall, the more likely they are to use the wall as an available resource. A teacher working with students in kindergarten and first grade might start with an ABC word wall of the names of all students in the class. Each day a child's name can be added to the list. Phonemic awareness, letter-name recognition, and letter-sound relationships (phonics) can be developed by asking students to count letters in the names that are listed, clap syllables, chant names of letters, and compare word length with other words shown on the word wall.

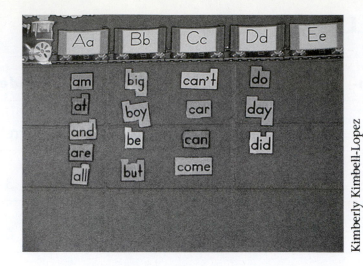

Kimberly Kimbell-Lopez

A–Application

After reading *If You Take a Mouse to School* by Laura Numeroff, the teacher tells students that the word *mouse* needs to be added to the class word wall. She asks students what sounds they hear in the word *mouse*—/m/ /ow/ /s/. She then repeats the word and writes down the letters on a word card, while also sounding out the word again. "We hear /m/ at the beginning of the word *mouse*, so what letter do I need to write to represent this sound? M." Once the word is spelled, the teacher asks students where the word should be placed on the word wall—in the section for *M* words. She then asks students what other words from the story they would like to write on the word wall. This process is repeated for each word added to the word wall.

The teacher also reinforces the strategy of cross-checking by selecting a word from the word wall and then giving students a clue to help them determine what word is missing from a given sentence.

- She writes the letter *c* on the board and says, "The missing word starts with *c*."
- She then gives this clue: "The _____ meowed at the door."
- She tells students to use the context of the sentence while also referring to the word wall for help with spelling. She asks them to write the word down (*cat*).
- She checks the answer by asking students to say the word and then read the sentence with the missing word. Next, they spell the word together.

This teacher does another activity with the word wall: she asks students to guess the word that is written down on a piece of paper by using four clues to figure out the word.

- "The word I have written down has four letters."
- "It starts with *w*."
- "The vowel is an *i*."
- "My word can be placed in the missing blank in this sentence: 'Go _____ me to the store.'"

The teacher always discusses with students the words that are added to the word wall. This helps reinforce their awareness of the words, and they can then use the word wall as a dictionary to help them when they need to spell words.

D–Delivery

The concept of a word wall is great for supporting learners in sight word development, but it is also a resource for other words explored in word study activities. Some suggestions for word study are given by Cunningham (2005), Gunning (2008), and Hall and Cunningham (1999):

1. Arrange words by rime so that all words containing that rime appear together in the list.
2. Color-code vowels in words in order to help identify vowel sounds. For example, write vowels with the short a sound in a red color.
3. Group words by category, such as colors, animals, numbers, and so on.
4. Ask students to locate opposites found on the wall. For example, ask them to find the opposite of *front*, which would be *back*.
5. Include a word on the wall that represents each of these beginning sounds: /sh/, /ch/, /th/, and /wh/.
6. With younger students, try to avoid introducing words in the same week that start with the same letter.
7. Include words that have these letter combinations somewhere within the word: *ch, sh, th, wh, qu, ph, wr, kn.*
8. Include words that have both sounds of *c* (/s/ and /k/), such as *ice* and *because,* as well as both sounds of *g* (/j/ and /g/), such as *good* and *huge.*
9. Include words that contain the most blends—*bl, br, cl, cr, dr, fl, fr, gr, pl, pr, sk, sl, sm, sn, sp, st,* and *tr.*
10. Introduce words that cover the most common vowel patterns. For example, the vowel *a* can be found in all these variations: *crash* (ă), *make* (ā), *rain* (ā), *played* (ā), *car* (är), *saw* (aw), and *caught* (ot).
11. List the most common contractions—*can't, didn't, don't, it's, they're,* and *won't.*
12. Recognize homophones—*to, too, two; there, their, they're; right, write; one, won; knew, new.*
13. Make sentences using words shown on the word wall.

References

Brabham, E. G., and S. K. Villaume. 2001. Building walls of words. *The Reading Teacher*, 54, 700–702.

Cunningham, P. M. 2005. *Phonics they use: Words for reading and writing.* 4th ed. New York: HarperCollins.

Gunning, T. G. 2008. *Creating literacy instruction for all children.* 6th ed. Boston: Allyn & Bacon.

Hall, D. P., and P. M. Cunningham. 1999. Multilevel word study: Word charts, word wall, and word sorts. In I. C. Fountas and G. S. Pinnell (Eds.). *Voices on word matters: Learning about phonics and spelling in the litearcy classroom* (pp. 114–130). Portsmouth, NH: Heinemann.

Section IV

Fluency

Fluency has, over the past several years, gained attention in regard to its role in the reading process. In its broadest sense, *fluency* refers to readers' mastery over the surface level of the text that they read—their ability to accurately and effortlessly decode the written words and then to give meaning to those words through appropriate phrasing and oral expression of the words (Rasinski 2007).

Proficient readers can identify words both accurately and rapidly. This ability to read with automaticity (Samuels 2006) frees cognitive resources to concentrate more on comprehension. Fluency is the essential element that helps bridge decoding (phonemic awareness and phonics) and meaning (vocabulary and comprehension).

For students who are beginning readers, it is not uncommon for them to read more slowly as they decode the text. However, students who are more proficient should be moving towards reading with automatic word recognition and prosody (i.e., intonation, stress, tempo, and phrasing). Students who read with fluency tend not to have issues with word recognition, which might cause them to pause, sound out a word, reread, or read ahead to identify the word. Any decoding required on the part of these students is done rapidly and without effort, and their attention is primarily on gaining meaning from the text.

Fluency is a reading skill that is often neglected in classroom instruction, yet it plays an important role in the reading process. Promoting fluent reading in the classroom requires explicit and strategic teaching, as do other elements of literacy instruction. Rasinski (2003) outlines four basic principles that underlie effective fluency instruction:

1. Modeling of fluent reading by the teacher or other fluent readers.
2. Providing oral support for students while they themselves read.
3. Practicing repeated readings of a given text.
4. Focusing attention on reading syntactically appropriate and meaningful phrases.

These basic principles are fluency building blocks that can be used for instruction and can be combined to create synergistic instructional routines (Rasinski 2003, 207). Fluency instruction conducted in short daily lessons (ten to fifteen minutes) best promotes the development of fluent readers.

References

Rasinski, T. V. 2003. *The fluent reader: Oral reading strategies for building word recognition, fluency, and comprehension.* New York: Scholastic.

Rasinski, T. V. 2007. Fluency: An oft-neglected goal of the reading program. In *Understanding and implementing Reading First initiatives: The changing role of administrators*, ed. C. Cummins, 60–71. Newark, DE: International Reading Association.

Samuels, S. J. 2006. Towards a model of reading fluency. In *What research has to say about fluency instruction*, ed. S. J. Samuels and A. E. Farstrup, 24–46. Newark, DE: International Reading Association.

CHORAL READING

When to Teach		Group Size		Grade Level	
Before Reading		One-on-One	👥	PreK–2	🏫
During Reading	📖	Small Group	👥	3–5	🏫
After Reading		Whole Group	👥	6–8	🏫

R–Rationale

Choral reading involves the teacher and students in reading a passage together in unison (Samuels 2006). The benefit of choral reading is that the teacher can model voice intonation and expression when reading a segment aloud first. Students are then able to emulate this intonation and expression when they read it aloud together.

E–Explanation

Choral reading is a form of repeated reading; students practice reading a text over and over with teacher guidance and support. The teacher can read the text first to students, and then they all read it again together. The teacher can also break the class into groups, with each group taking turns reading segments of the text. Throughout this process, the teacher continues to model how to read fluently (i.e., with expression, intonation, inflection).

A–Application

The teacher reads aloud to students the nursery rhyme "Ladybug, Ladybug."

> *Ladybug Ladybug*
> *Fly away home.*
> *Your house is on fire.*
> *And your children all gone.*
> *All except one,*
> *And that's little Ann,*
> *For she has crept under*
> *The frying pan.*

The teacher then tells students they are going to read the nursery rhyme again with a slight variation. He divides the class in half and asks one half to read the odd-numbered lines and the other half to read the even-numbered lines. The teacher has placed numbers beside the lines so that students can keep up with the lines they are to read. The teacher gives each section of students a few minutes to practice its lines. He then starts off by stating the title of the nursery rhyme again—"Ladybug, Ladybug." The first group then starts reading, and the second group follows. The reading continues until the nursery rhyme is finished.

The teacher then divides the nursery rhyme in half with four lines for each group. Again he gives students time to practice their lines before doing the choral reading. The first group then reads the beginning four lines, followed by the second group with the remaining lines. The teacher reads along with each group to model how to read with expression. This also helps them to keep their pace and to stay together.

D–Delivery

Nursery rhymes, poems, and songs work well for this kind of activity because they are not too long. The passage should also be on grade level for the students.

1. Select one of several options for reading the text:
   a. Read the text aloud together with the students.
   b. Read major sections alone, with students joining in on a chorus or refrain.
   c. Ask boys and girls to alternate lines.
   d. Divide the class into sections, and ask each section to be responsible for specific lines.
2. Read the text using the option selected. Be sure to model voice inflection and intonation for the students. So that students are shown what it means to be a fluent reader.
3. Continue reading the nursery rhyme using different variations. Repeated readings of the same text help students to develop fluency as readers.

Reference

Samuels, S. J. 2006. Towards a model of reading fluency. In *What research has to say about fluency instruction*, ed. S. J. Samuels and A. E. Farstrup, 24–46. Newark, DE: International Reading Association.

ECHO READING

When to Teach		Group Size		Grade Level	
Before Reading		One-on-One	👥	PreK–2	🏫
During Reading	📖	Small Group	👥	3–5	🏫
After Reading		Whole Group	👥	6–8	

R–Rationale

Echo reading is a strategy in which students listen to a skilled reader and then read the same segment of text, emulating the way it was read by the skilled reader. Echo reading is another type of assisted reading that can benefit students who are reading below grade level (Palumbo and Willcutt, 2006).

E–Explanation

Echo reading provides a support system for beginning readers to help them gain confidence when reading aloud. It is a way to help students read material that might at first appear to be too difficult. However, with teacher support, modeling, and guidance, the students gain the confidence they need to read it alone. They also have a chance to try out the voice inflection and intonation they have heard the skilled reader use.

A–Application

The major goal of echo reading is to have students emulate a skilled reader. In a similar approach to that of choral reading, the teacher uses short segments of texts for echo reading. For example, this teacher uses the following nursery rhyme:

> *Eeny, meeny, miny, moe,*
> *Catch a tiger by the toe.*
> *If he hollers let him go,*
> *Eeny, meeny, miny, moe.*
> *My mother told me*
> *To pick the very best one,*
> *And you are [not] it.*

The teacher first reads aloud the complete nursery rhyme from start to finish to give students an opportunity to hear it completely before they attempt the echo reading. The teacher takes a minute to talk about what the poem means, asking the students if they have ever used this rhyme to play games. Next, she reads aloud the first line and then pauses to let students read the line. Once they have finished, the teacher reads the next line and pauses again to allow students to read the line. She continues this process until the end of the nursery rhyme, modeling voice intonation and inflection as each line is read. If students do well reading line by line, the teacher repeats the process, reading two lines at a time instead of one.

D–Delivery

Echo reading is another form of repeated reading in which the teacher first reads a segment of text and the students then echo what was read.

1. Read a sentence or phrase aloud to students, reading with intonation and inflection to model what it means to read with expression.
2. As you read, track the text for emergent readers to reinforce the one-to-one correspondence between the spoken word and the written word.
3. Have the students then read the sentence or phrase back to you.
4. Repeat this process for each sentence or segment of text.

Reference

Palumbo, T. J., and J. R. Willcutt. 2006. In *What research has to say about fluency instruction*, ed. S. J. Samuels and A. E. Farstrup, 159–78. Newark, DE: International Reading Association.

FLUENCY DEVELOPMENT LESSON

When to Teach		Group Size		Grade Level	
Before Reading		One-on-One		PreK–2	🏫
During Reading	📖	Small Group	👥	3–5	🏫
After Reading		Whole Group	👥	6–8	🏫

R–Rationale

A fluency development lesson, or FDL (Rasinski et al. 1994), integrates several of the principles of effective fluency instruction within one lesson: modeling fluent reading, giving oral support to students as they read, practicing repeated readings of a text, and focusing on specific prosodic elements while reading. An FDL is designed to help students read smoothly with appropriate intonation.

E–Explanation

FDLs are daily ten- to fifteen-minute lessons designed to target the essential elements of fluency: speed, accuracy, and prosody. These minilessons involve a systematic process of modeled and practiced reading with a focus on a specific fluency element. The text to be used should be short and can be in any format (e.g., poetry, charts, short stories). All students should have a copy of the text or at least be able to clearly see the text during all aspects of the lesson.

A–Application

The teacher chooses a selection to be shared in the lesson. While the teacher reads, the students listen carefully and follow along silently. After the reading, the teacher and the students have a short discussion regarding elements of the reading: changes in the reader's tone, volume, pace, and so on. For example, in the poem "The Puffin" the students notice that the teacher slowed down and emphasized the words *bright*, *blue*, *sea*. They also notice that a change in his voice occurred when the puffin "cried for awhile." Next, the students read the poem chorally as a group, paying attention to the previously discussed prosodic elements. Students then engage in repeated readings with partners, providing support and encouragement to each other.

D–Delivery

An FDL uses short segments of passages that students can reread multiple times.

1. Conduct short, daily FDLs (five to 10 minutes) rather than one longer lesson per week.
2. Select a brief passage (50–200 words) to be read.

3. Make individual copies of the passage for students, or make a large copy that all students can easily see and read.
4. Read the passage aloud fluently while students listen.
5. Briefly discuss the passage, and point out, with the help of the students, places in the text which you read differently (e.g., louder or slower).
6. Reread the passage with students paying attention to the identified "fluency points."
7. Have students read the text with you, trying to mimic your reading. The reading can be done in a variety of forms (e.g., choral, antiphonal, echo).
8. Have students work with a partner to practice reading, providing appropriate support, encouragement, and feedback to one another.

Reference

Rasinski, T., N. Padak, W. Linek, and E. Sturtevant. 1994. Effects of fluency development on urban second-grade readers. *Journal of Educational Research* 87: 158–65.

NEUROLOGICAL IMPRESS METHOD

When to Teach		Group Size		Grade Level	
Before Reading		One-on-One	👥	PreK–2	🏫
During Reading	📖	Small Group		3–5	
After Reading		Whole Group		6–8	

R–Rationale

The neurological impress method (Heckelman 1969) provides oral support to a reader. The strategy involves regular intense reading sessions designed to help students become more fluent in their reading—that is, faster, more accurate, and more expressive.

E–Explanation

The neurological impress method (NIM) is similar in many ways to paired reading: a student reads orally and at the same time with a partner who acts as a tutor. The partner reader should be a more proficient reader in order to support and guide the less proficient student during the reading. The more proficient reader sits to the left and slightly behind the other student as both students read the text together. However, the more proficient reader reads slightly faster and louder than the other student and makes a conscious effort to direct her voice into the other student's left ear to "imprint" a sound-symbol match in that student's head. Because this type of one-on-one reading can be intense, initial NIM lessons should last only a few minutes, and even later sessions should not last more than ten to fifteen minutes.

A–Application

The teacher who is trying to help a student improve his reading fluency pairs him with a more proficient reader to read a selection from Shel Silverstein using NIM. Student A is the struggling reader, and Student B is the more proficient reader. The two students find two chairs in the back of the room and select the passage they want to read. Student B positions himself in a chair to the left and slightly behind Student A. The students then begin reading the text. Student B reads at a slightly faster rate than Student A, while directing his voice directly into Student A's left ear. This allows Student A to follow Student B's lead as needed. The students reread the text several times, paying attention to their rate of reading, their accuracy, and the appropriate use of prosody (i.e., tone, volume, phrasing).

D-Delivery

NIM is a strategy teachers can use to provide oral support to a reader.

1. Select, or have students select, a text to be read. The text should be at the less proficient student's instructional reading level and should relate to either a topic being studied or the reader's interest.
2. Pair students for the reading assignment, being sure that one reader is more proficient in order to support the other reader and model fluent reading.
3. Let the students select a spot for reading that allows the proficient reader to sit to the left and slightly behind the other reader.
4. Have the students read the text together, with the more proficient reader reading slightly faster and louder into the left ear of the other student.
5. Have them read the text multiple times, but the entire session should not exceed fifteen minutes.

Reference

Heckelman, R. G. 1969. A neurological impress method of reading instruction. *Academic Therapy* 4: 277–82.

READERS' THEATER

When to Teach		Group Size		Grade Level	
Before Reading	📖	One-on-One		PreK–2	🏫
During Reading	📖	Small Group	👥	3–5	🏫
After Reading	📖	Whole Group	👥	6–8	🏫

R–Rationale

Readers' theater is an interpretive reading activity in which students read from a script and use their voices to bring the characters in the script to life (Martinez, Roser, and Strecker 1998/1999). This activity involves students in reading a script multiple times as a way to develop fluency in reading as well as oral expressiveness and content-appropriate intonations and inflections. The readers' theater format gives "students a real-life reason to do repeated readings" (Samuels 2006, 30).

E–Explanation

The readers' theater format is an ideal way for students to participate in repeated readings in a meaningful and purposeful context, because students rehearse a script numerous times before reading it in a final performance (Martinez, Roser, and Strecker 1998/1999). Students read aloud from scripts, dramatizing through vocal and facial expressions but with minimal use of actions and props. Younger students enjoy using masks for readers' theater, which can easily be made from generic white paper plates that students color or decorate with crepe paper, construction paper, ribbon, or other materials. Teachers should allow time during the week for these students to create their masks. In addition, teachers should discuss with students the following guidelines for their performance:

- Read the script slowly, loudly, and with feeling.
- Keep the script down and away from your face so that you can be clearly heard.
- Face the audience when speaking so that you can be clearly heard.
- Use voice intonation and inflection to emphasize key parts of the script.
- Do not be distracted if someone in the audience talks or someone walks into the room during your practice or even your performance.
- If you mess up a line in the script, just keep going; act like it was meant to happen.
- If the audience laughs at something that happens in the script, pause a minute before continuing to read.

A–Application

In the script for *The Little Red Hen*, major parts include the narrator, the red hen, the dog, the pig, and the cow. A small group of five students can each take a role, or two to three students can share a part, either taking turns reading specific lines or reading the lines together in the style of choral reading. The teacher can suggest that students add sound effects as they read the script, such as animal sounds for the individual characters. The teacher allows the students to practice the script over two to three days and then schedules time for the group to present its readers' theater to the rest of the class.

D–Delivery

Readers' theater is a form of creative drama that reinforces students' skills as they read a script multiple times.

1. Select a script(s) that offer a variety of roles for students.
2. Introduce the scripts to students.
3. Allow students to decide which script they want to work on, and then form a small group to practice the script. In some cases, students will need to decide who will have which roles or whether any roles should be shared.
4. Provide students with thirty-minute time blocks for several days to practice their script together.
5. Coach the students on how to vary their voice level and pitch to portray the designated characters.
6. Allow students to present the script to an audience, such as another class, parents, or a school assembly.

References

Martinez, M., N. L. Roser, and S. Strecker. 1998/1999. "I never thought I could be a star": A Reader's Theatre ticket to fluency. *The Reading Teacher* 52: 326–34.

Samuels, S. J. 2006. Towards a model of reading fluency. In *What research has to say about fluency instruction*, ed. S. J. Samuels and A. E. Farstrup, 24–46. Newark, DE: International Reading Association.

TAPE-ASSISTED READING

When to Teach		Group Size		Grade Level	
Before Reading		One-on-One	👥	PreK–2	🏫
During Reading	📖	Small Group	👥	3–5	🏫
After Reading		Whole Group		6–8	🏫

R–Rationale

Tape-assisted reading, also known as recorded reading or talking books (Carbo 1978), allows students to follow the text while working on phrasing, fluency, and comprehension. This strategy can be used to provide repeated readings for students who need fluency practice and to break down barriers for intimidated beginning readers.

E–Explanation

Tape-assisted reading is a fluency strategy that provides students with auditory reinforcement combined with the visual image of print. The focus of this strategy can be on reading for pleasure or for improving fluency and comprehension. Through recorded books, students can read and reread stories while hearing what a fluent reader sounds like. It is important to remind students that when participating in tape-assisted reading, they must read the text to themselves as they listen. It is the repeated reading of the text that improves fluency, not just listening to the story.

Tapes of stories can be purchased, but it is often easier and more cost efficient for teachers to create their own. This improves the chance that the voice on the tape is not culturally different from that of the students and also allows teachers to match the reading rates of their students. Parent volunteers and older students can assist in reading stories onto tapes to be used in the classroom.

A–Application

After sharing the story *Corduroy* with the class during read-aloud time, the teacher creates an audiotape of the story. The tape and book are kept in the reading center so that students can listen as they reread the story.

D–Delivery

Tape-assisted reading provides students with multiple exposures to good books. This repeated reading improves their fluency, comprehension, and vocabulary while instilling a love for reading.

1. Purchase and/or create audiotapes of books. Since students will have the support of a proficient reader reading with them, the books can be at a slightly higher level than the students' instructional level. Select stories for tape-assisted reading that are of high interest to the students.
2. Introduce the story to the class, and provide the initial reading in a read-aloud or shared reading format.
3. Discuss the story with students, making sure that they have a good understanding of the story.
4. Place the book and accompanying audiotape in the tape-assisted reading center for additional readings and exploration.

Reference

Carbo, M. 1978. Teaching reading with talking books. *The Reading Teacher* 35: 186–89.

Section V

Vocabulary

Vocabulary development is defined as "the growth of a person's stack of known words and meanings" and "the teaching-learning principles and practices that lead to such growth" (Harris and Hodges 1995, 275). It is estimated that students learn 2,000 to 3,000 or more new words each year. This means that a child learns an average of seven words per day. By the end of high school, students could have learned more than 24,000 new words.

Surprisingly, most of these words are learned outside of explicit classroom instruction. Incidental learning of vocabulary from context contributes a large amount of students' vocabulary growth (Nagy, Herman, and Anderson 1985; Nagy and Scott 2004). Only a fraction of the words are learned through focused vocabulary activities.

The amount of time spent reading also contributes to vocabulary growth. A child who is reading well will continue to show growth in vocabulary. This phenomenon is called the Matthew Effect (based on a parable in the Gospel of Matthew in the Bible), which means that the rich get richer (i.e., those who can read become better readers) and the poor get poorer (i.e., those who struggle with reading fall behind in vocabulary growth and therefore in reading) (Stanovich 2004).

Although vocabulary is often gained through incidental exposure, explicit instruction is also needed. The importance of vocabulary instruction was addressed in the report from the National Reading Panel (2000), which emphasized that vocabulary instruction can lead to gains in reading comprehension. The larger a student's vocabulary, the easier it is to make sense of a text. If a word is not in a student's oral vocabulary, the word will not likely be understood when it is read in print.

Explicit, strategic instruction helps build a student's reservoir of words. We must help students to develop an in-depth knowledge of words through rich vocabulary instruction that provides a combination of direct instruction along with opportunities for wide reading and other forms of incidental exposure. A teacher should consider the following ideas when planning vocabulary instruction (Carr & Wixson 1986; Kameenui, Carnine, and Freschi 1982; McKeown & Beck 2004; Nagy and Herman 1987; National Reading Panel 2000; Snow 2003; Stahl 1986; Stahl and Fairbanks 1986):

1. All words are not of equal importance; students should be taught words they will encounter often in print.
2. Core words that represent major aspects of the English language should be taught (i.e., high frequency words, words with special word parts, words that sound alike).
3. Opportunities for wide reading should be provided so that students can encounter a substantial number of unfamiliar words. Reading opportunities should include a variety of methods (e.g., read-aloud, shared reading, guided reading, literature circles, independent reading) as well as a variety of materials (e.g., trade books, magazines, newspapers, comic books).
4. Instruction should move beyond the memorization of definitions as the way to learn words. Teaching definitions is not as effective as exposing students to words in many contexts.

5. Students need multiple exposures to a new word and its meaning. Students must be able to decode the word during reading to help access the meaning automatically. To do this, students must have many opportunities to encounter the new word.
6. Strategies must target how to infer word meaning from the context. Students must be taught to recognize different categories of context clues that may be encountered in texts (e.g., background experience, definitions, examples, comparison/contrast, and word function), and they must use these clues to help determine the meanings of words.
7. Connecting vocabulary to students' background is important. Teachers should help students relate new words to what they already know by providing opportunities to explore relationships between words.
8. Students should be actively involved in using a new word and concept in context. It is important that we move away from teaching vocabulary words in isolation.
9. Instruction should be planned to facilitate the development of elaborated word knowledge. Vocabulary instruction should move students beyond the simple memorization of a definition and use in a single context. Students should consider how to use words in different situations while exploring relationships between words.

Vocabulary plays a vital role in every aspect of reading. The goal of vocabulary instruction should be to help students learn vocabulary words in such a way that they will retain their knowledge and understanding of the vocabulary words and the relationships of those words with other words.

References

Carr, E., and K. K. Wixson. 1986. Guidelines for evaluating vocabulary instruction. *Journal of Reading* 29: 588–95.

Harris, T. L., and R. E. Hodges. 1995. *The literacy dictionary: The vocabulary of reading and writing*. Newark, DE: International Reading Association.

Kameenui, E. J., D. W. Carnine, and R. Freschi. 1982. Effects of text construction and instructional procedure for teaching word meanings on comprehension and recall. *Reading Research Quarterly* 17(3): 367–88.

McKeown, M. G., and I. L. Beck. 2004. Direct and rich vocabulary instruction. In *Vocabulary instruction: Research to practice*, ed. J. F. Baumann and E. J. Kameenui, 13–27. New York: Guilford.

Nagy, W., and P. Herman. 1987. Breadth and depth of vocabulary knowledge: Implications for acquisition and instruction. In *The nature of vocabulary acquisition*, ed. M. G. McKeown and M. E. Curtis, 19–35, Hillsdale, NJ: Lawrence Erlbaum.

Nagy, W. E., P. Herman, and R. C. Anderson. 1985. Learning words from contect. *Reading Research Quarterly* 20: 233–53.

Nagy, W. E., and J. A. Scott. 2004. Vocabulary processes. In. R. B. Ruddell and N. J. Unrau (eds.). *Theoretical models and processes of reading* (5th ed.), 574–93. Newark, DE: International Reading Association.

National Reading Panel. 2000. *Teaching children to read: An evidence-based assessment of the scientific research literature on reading and its implications for reading instruction* (NIH Publication No. 00-4769). Washington, DC: National Institute of Child Health and Human Development, National Institute of Health.

Snow, C. 2003. Assessment of reading comprehension: Researchers and practitioners helping themselves and each other. In *Rethinking reading comprehension*, ed. A. Sweet and C. Snow, 254–69. New York: Guilford.

Stahl, S. A. 1986. Three principles of effective vocabulary instruction. *Journal of Reading* 29: 662–69.

Stahl, S. A., and M. M. Fairbanks. 1986. The effects of vocabulary instruction: A model-based meta-analysis. *Review of Educational Research* 56: 72–81.

Stanovich, K. E. 2004. Matthew effects in reading: Some consequences of individual differences in acquisition of literacy. In R. B. Ruddell and N. J. Unrau. (eds). *Theoretical models and processes of reading* (5th ed.), 454–516. Newark, DE: International Reading Association.

CONCEPT CIRCLES

When to Teach		Group Size		Grade Level	
Before Reading	📖	One-on-One	👥	PreK–2	🏫
During Reading		Small Group	👥	3–5	🏫
After Reading	📖	Whole Group	👥	6–8	🏫

R–Rationale

Concept circles are a type of graphic organizer in which students associate related words to a key topic or vocabulary word. The key word is placed above or below the larger circle, and associated words are placed inside the circle. The goal of concept circles is for students to relate words conceptually (Vacca and Vacca 2002). This type of strategy encourages students to categorize words by either identifying an overall label shared by the listed elements, identifying missing elements in a concept circle, or identifying the element that does not belong in a concept circle.

E–Explanation

Students are given a circle divided into parts with words or phrases written in most or all of the sections. They must decide what relationship exists among the parts of the concept circle. They can identify an overall category, a missing part, or a part that is not correctly included.

A–Application

Concept circles can be used for most grade levels. In the first example shown below, all of the sections relate to tornadoes. The teacher asks the students to review the parts that are included in the concept circle and then decide what overall topic or category is related to those parts.

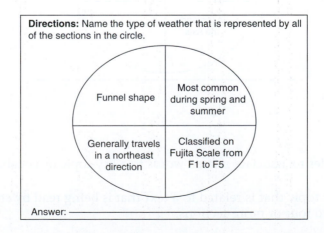

Directions: Name the type of weather that is represented by all of the sections in the circle.

Funnel shape

Most common during spring and summer

Generally travels in a northeast direction

Classified on Fujita Scale from F1 to F5

Answer: _____

A variation on the concept circle identifies the concept but includes one part in the circle that does not belong. The concept circle below describes aspects of hurricanes. The part that does not belong is "rotate in a clockwise direction" since hurricanes actually rotate in a counterclockwise direction.

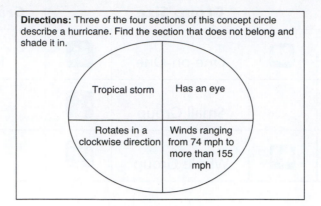

Directions: Three of the four sections of this concept circle describe a hurricane. Find the section that does not belong and shade it in.

Tropical storm | Has an eye

Rotates in a clockwise direction | Winds ranging from 74 mph to more than 155 mph

In a third variation the teacher leaves one section of the concept circle blank. Students are to use the information available in the three parts of the concept circle to determine the topic of the concept circle. Then they complete the fourth, blank part of the circle by filling in an additional piece of information about the topic. For example, three of the sections of a concept circle might be the following:

- Rocky, metallic objects
- Sometimes known as minor planets
- Include Toutatis, Castalia, Geographos, and Vesta

Based on this information, students would decide that the answer is asteroids. They would then complete the missing section with another piece of information about asteroids. In the example below, once students have identified the topic as World War II, their challenge would be to research other information to complete the fourth part of the circle.

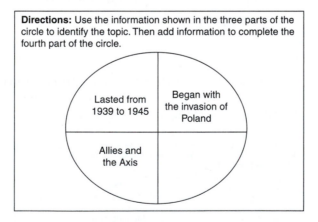

Directions: Use the information shown in the three parts of the circle to identify the topic. Then add information to complete the fourth part of the circle.

Lasted from 1939 to 1945 | Began with the invasion of Poland

Allies and the Axis |

D–Delivery

Students use concept circles to associate related words to a key topic or vocabulary word.

1. Identify a specific topic that is related to a text that is being read by students.
2. Divide a circle into four or more sections.

3. Identify words or phrases related to the topic.
4. Decide what type of concept circle will be used:
   a. Circle with all four parts filled in. Students must identify the overall topic.
   b. Circle with all four parts filled in, but one part does not belong. Students must decide which part does not fit the topic.
   c. Circle with the topic missing and three parts of the circle filled in. Students must complete the missing part of the circle and identify the topic.
   d. Circle with sections filled in and topic missing. Students must review the information and identify the topic of discussion
5. Model for students how to work with a concept circle by using the clues that are given.
6. Provide each student with a copy of a concept circle. Let students work with a partner or in small groups to find the answers for the concept circles.
7. Bring the class back together as a whole group, and discuss what answers they have identified for each concept circle.

Reference

Vacca, R. T. and J. L. Vacca. 2002. *Content area reading.* 7th ed. Boston: Allyn & Bacon.

CONTEXT CLUES

When to Teach		Group Size		Grade Level	
Before Reading		One-on-One		PreK–2	
During Reading		Small Group		3–5	
After Reading		Whole Group		6–8	

R–Rationale

Context clues refer to how a word is used in the text. Students can learn to use different categories of context clues to identify the meaning of an unfamiliar word they encounter in a text. Effective vocabulary instruction should provide both adequate definitions and illustrations of how the words are used in a natural context or within a text (Nagy 1988).

E–Explanation

Context clues are only helpful if there is enough information available to determine the meaning. Consider the following sentence:

> Stella is very tall, while Kristen is more *petite*.

To understand the word *petite* in this sentence, the child needs more information than is available in the rest of the sentence. We can help move students beyond a partial and incomplete understanding of vocabulary words by providing classroom experiences that teach them how to use words meaningfully.

Teachers can show students how to use context to identify word meanings by recognizing specific categories of context clues that might be encountered in texts. These clues can include background experience, definitions, examples, comparison/contrast, and word function.

A–Application

The teacher selects a short passage from a book or a poem and then covers up a major vocabulary word in the text. In this example, the teacher chooses a short excerpt from Megan McDonald's *Judy Moody Saves the World* (2002) in which the teacher, Mr. Todd, is giving the class an assignment:

> "If we want to take care of our planet, it helps to begin in our own backyard. That's why I'm asking each of you to adopt an _____ animal from Virginia this week. Tell us about the species, why it's disappearing and what can be done to help."

The teacher reads the passage to the students and then asks them what clues they can get from the reading, such as these:

- taking care of our planet
- animals are disappearing
- how we can help

Next, she makes a list of possible words the students think would fit and then has them narrow down the choices to just one word. Once students have made their decision, she discusses with them how closely it matches the actual word—*endangered*.

D–Delivery

Teachers can show students how to use different categories of context clues to identify the meaning of an unfamiliar word they encounter in a text.

1. Select a passage from a book or other text that the class has been reading. Identify vocabulary words in the passage that students need to learn to understand the story or context.
2. Display the passage on chart paper, an overhead, or other means of projection. Read the passage to students but say "blank" for the missing word.
3. After the passage is read, ask students to look at the first blank. Read the sentence again.
4. Ask students to talk with a partner about what the missing word might be. Discuss as a class the words students think would fit in the blank. Ask them what clues they found in the text that helped them to determine the word (definition, example, and so on).
5. Once the students make a final decision about the missing word, continue through the passage, following this same process.
6. Compare the completed passage with the actual passage from the book to see how well students used context clues. If their words did not match, talk about whether there was any similarity between their answer and the correct answer. For example, was the word they selected a synonym for the word used by the author, or were they completely off base with their word choice? If they were off base, go back to that sentence, and talk about what they could have done differently to select a word that was appropriate.

Six Categories of Context Clues

Category	Description	Example Sentence
Background Experience	Students draw on their own experiences to figure out the meaning of a word. In the example passage about different types of dinosaurs, students can draw on their knowledge of an army tank to infer that the Ankylosaurus was large and covered with armor.	*"**Ankylosaurus** was the size of an army tank—and built like one! Its body and head were covered with armor. The armor was made of bone. It protected Ankylosaurus from flesh-eating dinosaurs like T. Rex."* (Osborne and Obsorne 2000, 70)
Definitions	A definition of the word is included in the text. In the example, the word *regret* is followed by a description of what it means to regret something that was done.	*"One of the most difficult things to think about in life is one's **regrets**. Something will happen to you, and you will do the wrong thing, and for years afterward you will wish you had done something different."* (Snicket 1999, 43)
Examples	Specific examples of what the word means are included in the surrounding context. In the excerpt here, Junie gives several examples of her gleeful behavior.	*"My Grampa Miller really did buy me mittens for no reason! And they are gorgeous, I tell you! When I first opened them, I got filled with **glee**. Glee is when you run. And jump. And skip. And laugh. And clap. And dance on top of the dining room table."* Park 1997, 2–3)
Comparison/Contrast	The word is compared or contrasted with one or more words that help to determine the meaning of the unknown word.	*"Although it was cold in the attic, she could feel the **radiant** warmth of the day; her skin drank the loveliness of the sun."* (L'Engle 1978, 59)
Word Function	Readers can get clues from how a word is used—for example, as a noun, verb, adjective, or adverb. Using *chisel* as a noun helps students realize it is a tool.	*"Using only copper **chisels** and wooden hammers, the workers slowly carved the stone blocks."* (Simon 2003, 28)

References

L'Engle, M. 1978. *A swiftly tilting planet.* New York: Bantam Doubleday Dell.

McDonald, M. 2002. *Judy Moody saves the world!* Cambridge, MA: Candlewick Press.

Nagy, W. E. 1988. *Teaching vocabulary to improve reading instruction.* Newark, DE: International Reading Association.

Osborne, W., and M. P. Osborne. 2000. *Magic tree house research guide: Dinosaurs.* New York: Scholastic.

Park, B. 1997. *Junie B. Jones is not a crook.* New York: Random House.

Simon, S. 2003. *Pyramids and mummies.* New York: Scholastic.

Snicket, L. 1999. *A series of unfortunate events: The reptile room.* New York: HarperCollins.

FRAYER MODEL

When to Teach		Group Size		Grade Level	
Before Reading	📖	One-on-One	👤	PreK–2	
During Reading		Small Group	👥	3–5	🏫
After Reading	📖	Whole Group	👥	6–8	🏫

R–Rationale

The Frayer model (Frayer, Frederick, and Klausmeier 1969) is a strategy that actively engages students in analyzing a word beyond the parameters of a definition. It allows students an opportunity to think and talk about words in order to truly develop an understanding of a word.

E–Explanation

This strategy is used to help students understand a word or concept by studying it from four different yet relational perspectives. Students use a four-square graphic organizer to help complete the word analysis process. They analyze the word first by identifying essential and nonessential characteristics and then refine their understanding by choosing examples and nonexamples to represent the word or concept.

A–Application

While planning instruction for a unit on volcanoes, a fourth-grade teacher realizes that students might not be familiar with the word *dormant*. Instead of having the students simply look the word up in the dictionary, he uses the Frayer model to allow them to derive their own definition. The teacher can draw the Frayer model chart on the board, reproduce it for individual students, or have students create their own by folding a sheet of paper in half longwise, folding it again in the other direction, and then finding the common corner of the fold and turning it down about an inch. When the paper is opened, the folds will have produced four squares with a diamond shape in the middle for the target word. The teacher then has students label the four squares: definition, characteristics, examples, and nonexamples. He allows students to use the dictionary to look up the word if needed to generate a discussion. Once the word is discussed, the teacher has the students create their own student-friendly definition to be recorded on the chart. He then has them further analyze the definition in order to identify key characteristics, examples, and nonexamples that will help them better understand the term. Once this deeper analysis of the word is complete, the teacher has students revisit their definition and make revisions as needed.

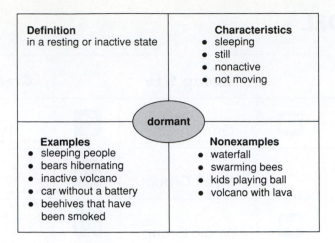

D–Delivery

Initially, this strategy should be presented via explicit modeling and think-alouds by the teacher. However, once students understand the four attributes being analyzed in the modeled lessons, the strategy can be used independently or in small groups.

1. Draw the Frayer model graphic organizer on the board, pass out individual copies, or have students create their own—a rectangle divided into four equal sections with a large oval or diamond in the middle.
2. Label the four sections left-to-right and top-to-bottom: Definition, Characteristics, Examples, Nonexamples.
3. Pronounce the word to be studied, and write it in the middle section of the graphic organizer.
4. Conduct a quick general discussion of the word, and then work collaboratively with students to come up with a general, student-friendly definition of the word.
5. Analyze alone or with students, or have them analyze, the word from the three perspectives.
6. Have students record their responses in the appropriate boxes as they work through each area of analysis. Be sure to always have students share the rationales for their responses.
7. Have students revisit and revise the initial student-friendly definition as needed.
8. Have students take turns using the new word in an appropriate context.
9. Consider including a section on the chart for students to provide an illustration of the target word as in the vocabulary cards strategy.

Reference

Frayer, D., W. C. Frederick, and H. J. Klausmeier. 1969. *A schema for testing the level of cognitive mastery*. Madison, WI: Wisconsin Center for Education Research.

LINEAR ARRAYS

When to Teach		Group Size		Grade Level	
Before Reading	📖	One-on-One	👥	PreK–2	
During Reading		Small Group	👥	3–5	🏫
After Reading	📖	Whole Group	👥	6–8	🏫

R–Rationale

Linear arrays refer to a group of words that are arranged in a linear format in order to show shades of meaning between the words. The words in a linear array can be arranged according to degree of size, frequency, intensity, position, or chronology. This strategy can be used to illustrate the connection between synonyms and antonyms by depicting gradations between two related words (Allen 1999).

E–Explanation

The linear array consists of five to six circles connected in a straight line. The middle circles are designed to show the subtle changes in meaning between the word on the extreme left and the word on the extreme right. Students can be given sets of words to place in order in a linear array—for example, *yesterday*, *present*, *future*, *past*, and *tomorrow*. The teacher can also give students parts of the array and ask them to find other words that would fit in the missing parts. A dictionary or thesaurus is a good source for finding words.

A–Application

In the example shown here, the words *incessant* and *rare* can be considered antonyms. The teacher shows *incessant* on the left side and *rare* on the right side and talks with students about the fact that the words are antonyms, which means they have opposite meanings. She also talks with them about what each word means. She then tells students their job is to decide how to arrange the other three words—*periodic*, *frequent*, and *scanty*. She talks with students about what each of the three words means and also what the words mean in relationship to *incessant* and *rare*. The teacher and the students decide together how the words should be placed in the linear array.

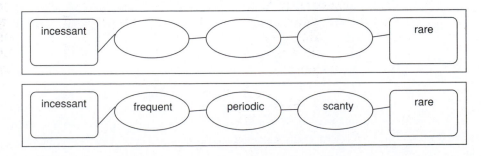

D–Delivery

Students can use linear arrays to show subtle changes in the meanings of words.

1. Select two words that are opposite in meaning.
2. Identify two or three words that are close in meaning to each word.
3. Select three or more of those words to arrange in the linear array.
4. Share the linear array with students, and model for them how to make decisions regarding the placement of each word.
5. Once students understand the process, give partners or small groups of students a linear array. Ask them to arrange the words in the linear array to show the changes in meaning as they move from one side of the array to the other side.
6. Bring the class back together as a whole group, and discuss how each group placed the words in the linear array.
7. As an additional challenge, let students create their own linear arrays, which could become part of a center activity to give students more opportunities to explore words.

Reference

Allen, J. 1999. *Words, words, words: Teaching vocabulary in grades 4–12*. Portland, ME: Stenhouse.

LIST-GROUP-LABEL

When to Teach		Group Size		Grade Level	
Before Reading	📖	One-on-One		PreK–2	🏫
During Reading		Small Group	👥	3–5	🏫
After Reading	📖	Whole Group	👥	6–8	🏫

R–Rationale

List-group-label (Taba 1967) is a brainstorming activity that helps students see how words can belong in a variety of groups and also activates and builds background knowledge prior to beginning a unit of study. This strategy stimulates thinking about a topic and strengthens students' ability to see patterns and relationships among topic-related items.

E–Explanation

List-group-label was originally developed to help students deal with technical vocabulary in content areas but actually helps students improve not only their vocabulary but also their categorization skills. This strategy stimulates thinking about a topic, then extends that thinking by analyzing and searching for topic-related patterns and relationships, and finally categorizes the words or concepts by identifying a representative label.

A–Application

A first-grade class is preparing for a unit on farm animals. To jumpstart the unit, to find out what background knowledge students already have about the classification of animals, and to provide students with an opportunity to practice looking for patterns and relationships, the teacher decides to use the list-group-label strategy. He places a piece of chart paper on the board and labels it animals. He then has the students brainstorm all the animals they know and records these on the chart.

List of Animals		
zebra	cow	possum
deer	mule	parrot
pig	antelope	blue jay
cat	lion	goldfish
horse	sheep	elephant
dog	goat	coyote
tiger	raccoon	giraffe

Once the list is complete, the teacher cuts the animal names apart. The class discusses the characteristics of the animals while collaboratively sorting the animal names based on relationships.

Animals Organized into Groups			
zebra	deer	cat	pig
tiger	possum	dog	horse
lion	raccoon	goldfish	cow
giraffe	coyote	parrot	mule
elephant	blue jay		sheep
antelope			goat

The students then view the newly formed animal categories and assign a label to each category.

Labeled Groups			
Jungle	**Forest/Woods**	**House**	**Farm**
zebra	deer	cat	pig
tiger	possum	dog	horse
lion	raccoon	goldfish	cow
giraffe	coyote	parrot	mule
elephant	blue jay		sheep
antelope			goat

D–Delivery

List-group-label allows students to activate and build prior knowledge before beginning a unit of study. This strategy helps students make connections in their minds as they search for patterns and relationships among topic-related items.

List

1. Provide students with a stimulus topic.
2. Have students brainstorm a list of words they associate with the topic. Consider whether to provide any words for the students; generally it is better if they generate the words.
3. Record the words on a chart, chalkboard, overhead, computer, or other surface. Lists for younger students may contain ten to fifteen words; for older students, twenty-five to thirty words. It is important that students provide a brief explanation of each word's connection to the topic.
4. Pronounce each word on the word list, and let students speculate about the meanings.

Group

5. Ask students to look for patterns and/or relationships among the words. It may be helpful to cut the words apart and/or duplicate them on index cards so that students can physically sort them.
6. Have students group the words based on the patterns and relationships. Write the words again on the chart, chalkboard, overhead, or other surface, but this time in their groups. Words can be used in more than one category as long as an explanation can be provided.

Label

7. Have students examine the newly created lists and name or label the categories, based on the relationships of the words.
8. If this activity precedes a unit of study, have students read the selection and then revisit the labeled groups, making additions/revisions as needed to reflect any new understandings.

Reference

Taba, H. 1967. *Teacher's handbook for elementary social studies*. Reading, MA: Addison-Wesley.

POSSIBLE SENTENCES

When to Teach		Group Size		Grade Level	
Before Reading		One-on-One		PreK–2	
During Reading		Small Group		3–5	
After Reading		Whole Group		6–8	

R–Rationale

Possible sentences (Moore and Moore 1986) is a strategy designed to help students determine independently the meanings and relationships of unfamiliar words in reading assignments. It also helps students understand the importance of activating prior knowledge about vocabulary prior to reading and of using the text to refine and revise their understandings while reading.

E–Explanation

Possible sentences is a strategy that helps students (1) learn new vocabulary to be encountered in a reading selection; (2) make predictions about a text's contents; (3) provide a purpose for reading; (4) become curious about the text to be read; and (5) present their ideas to one another, justify their ideas, listen to others' points of view, and evaluate their own understandings. It is a five-part lesson that provides students an opportunity to use all language processes as they learn new words: list key vocabulary, elicit sentences, read and verify sentences, evaluate sentences, and generate new sentences.

A–Application

A third grade teacher preparing a lesson that centers around a reading selection about volcanoes. She lists a number of terms that the students will encounter in their reading (i.e. dormant, surface, eruptions, and lava). Prior to introducing the text, the teacher asks students to select partners and gives each pair a couple of words. She asks the teams to write sentences that use the vocabulary words. Then volunteers from each team write the sentences on the chalkboard for the class to discuss. After the class discussions, the students read the assigned text. After seeing the words in the text, students are told to revisit their sentences to check for accuracy in the way the words were used. They are able to make changes in the sentences, if needed. Again, the teacher asks the students to write their sentences on the chalkboard for the class to discuss. She then has students record their sentences, or create new ones, in their vocabulary journals.

Initial Sentences	Revised Sentences
1. A dormant volcano is no threat to people living in the surrounding area.	1.
2. More than 80% of the earth's surface has come from volcanoes.	2.
3. One of the most devastating volcanic eruptions was Mt. St. Helens in southwest Washington State in 1980.	3.
4. Lava is a heavy substance that sinks to the bottom of a volcano.	4. Lava is a substance that flows out of a volcano when it erupts.

D–Delivery

The steps for possible sentences sometimes vary in number, but the important thing to remember is that it is a five-part lesson and that each of these five aspects should be present.

1. Write key vocabulary terms from the text on the chalkboard, chart paper, or overhead projector. Predetermine the words that are central to the main concepts in the text. Pronounce each word, and make sure that each word can be defined by using the text.
2. Ask students to select pairs of words from the list. For each pair, have students write a sentence that they think might appear in the text.
3. Ask student volunteers to write their sentences on the board, underlining the words they have included from the list.
4. Discuss the sentences. Ask if anyone disagrees with any of the sentences.
5. Have students read the text on their own to verify the accuracy of their sentences.
6. Discuss the sentences again as a class. Have students evaluate the sentences for accuracy, and ask students to make any changes they wish.
7. Ask students to create additional sentences, based on information from the text. This extends students' understanding of the meanings and relationships of the vocabulary words. As students generate new sentences, they should be checked against the text for accuracy.
8. Encourage students to record their sentences in their notebooks for further study.

Reference

Moore, D. W., and S. A. Moore. 1986. Possible sentences. In *Reading in the content areas: Improving classroom instruction* (2nd ed.), ed. E. K. Dishner, T. W. Bean, and J. E. Readence, 174–79. Dubuque, IA: Kendall Hunt.

PREDICT-O-GRAM

When to Teach		Group Size		Grade Level	
Before Reading	📖	One-on-One		PreK–2	🏫
During Reading		Small Group	👥	3–5	🏫
After Reading	📖	Whole Group	👥	6–8	🏫

R–Rationale

Predict-o-grams (Barr and Johnson 1997), also known as vocab-o-grams, are used to allow students to go beyond the definition of a word and consider its application in the text. This strategy also encourages students to form predictions about a selection, based on key words found in the text.

E–Explanation

Predict-o-grams allow students to make predictions based on the author's choice of words and to see how authors use specific words to tell a story. In addition to building vocabulary, this strategy enhances students' understanding of story elements.

A–Application

Prior to reading the story *Edward the Emu* by Sheena Knowles, the teacher lists on the chalkboard or overhead several words from the story, and students share their current understandings of the words. The teacher then puts the students in small groups and passes out the predict-o-gram template as shown on the next page.

Predict-o-Gram

Story title: _____	
New Vocabulary Words	
Setting	Which words tell you about when and where the story took place?
Characters	Which words tell you about the characters in the story?
Problem/Goal	Which words describe the problem or goal?
Action/Events	Which words tell you what might happen?
Resolution	Which words tell you how the story might end?
What question(s) do you have?	
Mystery words:	

Working collaboratively, each group makes predictions regarding where each vocabulary word might be found as it relates to the story structure. For example, the words *emu, seals,* and *lions* are placed in the character section of the template. The teacher also asks the students to make a prediction about how these characters might be involved in the story. Students continue until all words have been placed in a category on the template and predictions made. If students cannot decide on a category for a word, it can be temporarily placed in the mystery word category. The groups share their predictions and their rationales for each placement. Then the students listen as the teacher reads the story aloud to the class. After the story, students revisit their predictions for accuracy, make revisions if needed, and share their thoughts about the story and the ways the author used the chosen words. Part of a predict-o-gram for *Edward the Emu* is shown on the next page.

Predict-o-Gram
Edward the Emu

emu zookeeper	pen lion	roared replaced	bored seals
Setting pen zookeeper	**Which words tell you about when and where the story took place?** At the zoo.		
Characters emu lion seals	**Which words tell you about the characters in the story?** There are an emu, a lion, and some seals at a zoo.		
Problem/Goal bored replaced	**Which words describe the problem or goal?** One of the animals is bored, so they send him away and replace him with a different animal.		

D–Delivery

Predict-o-grams can be used as an individual, small group, or whole class activity. However, because the discussion helps facilitate understanding of both the vocabulary and the story structure, it is recommended that the strategy be used with a small or whole group.

1. Write a list of vocabulary words from the reading selection on the chalkboard, overhead, or chart. Be sure that the words reflect story structure in some way.
2. Discuss the meanings of the words with the class.
3. Distribute copies of the predict-o-gram template to the students, or draw the predict-o-gram on the board.
4. Have students use their knowledge of the new vocabulary words and story structure (i.e., setting, characters, problem, events, resolution) to predict each word's use in the story. Let students know that they can place a word in more than one category. If they have no idea where a word might fit, tell them to place it temporarily in the mystery words section.
5. Bring the whole group together, and have students share their placement of the words. Be sure to elicit students' knowledge about the words and strategies they used to predict meanings.
6. Have students return to the predict-o-gram and make predictions based on the placement of the words relative to the story structure.
7. Allow students time to read the text or listen to the text read-aloud, and then ask them to confirm or reject their earlier predictions. Consider having them rewrite their inaccurate predictions.
8. Return to the text, and discuss how the author used the words in the story.

Reference

Barr, R., and B. Johnson. 1997. *Teaching reading and writing in elementary classrooms.* 2nd ed. New York: Longman.

SEMANTIC FEATURE ANALYSIS

When to Teach		Group Size		Grade Level	
Before Reading	📖	One-on-One	👥	PreK–2	🏫
During Reading		Small Group	👪	3–5	🏫
After Reading	📖	Whole Group	👥👥	6–8	🏫

R–Rationale

The semantic feature analysis (SFA) activity uses a chart or grid to compare words or ideas. This approach takes advantage of how the brain organizes information (Johnson and Pearson 1984; Pittelman et al. 1991). It also reinforces vocabulary development, since it focuses on helping students identify whether a relationship exists between words and other features that have been identified.

E–Explanation

SFA presents information to students in a table format, and students determine whether a relationship exists between selected categories. Words are listed in the left column whereas criteria or features are listed across the top. Students have to decide whether each word in the left column is associated with the criteria across the top and indicate their decision with a plus or minus sign.

A–Application

In the example illustrated on the next page, students have to decide whether each animal listed in the left column has the feature listed in the top row. If they are not sure of the answer, the teacher encourages them to do further research using books and Internet resources. In this case, the students learn that crocodiles lay eggs, have a backbone, and are meat eaters, but they do not give birth to their young and do not eat plants or insects. When their charts are completed, the teacher discusses with the students what all of the animals have in common. This leads to an acknowledgment that they are all vertebrates, and the teacher challenges the students to find out other characteristics of vertebrates, as well as the category of vertebrate of each animal listed (e.g., mammal, fish, and so on).

Semantic Feature Analysis Chart

	Lays Eggs	Live Birth	Has a Backbone	Meat Eater	Plant Eater	Insect Eater
Crocodile	+	-	+	+	-	-
Horse	-	+	+	-	+	-
Frog	+	-	+	-	+	+
Bird	+	-	+	+	+	+
Goldfish	+	-	+	-	+	+

Teachers can also use the information from SFA charts to create analogies for students to complete.

crocodile : eggs   AS   horse : _____   (Answer: live birth)

goldfish : _____   AS   crocodile : meat-eater   (Answer: insect eater)

An SFA chart can help extend students' exploration of words by having them seek out possible relationships. Once students have done the activity with teacher support, they can then create their own SFA charts as part of classroom projects. These new charts can be challenges for other students in the class to complete.

D–Delivery

The SFA strategy uses a chart or grid format to show relationships among words.

1. Select a category, identify words related to the category, and list these words down the left side of a grid.
2. Determine what critical features or attributes are shared by the words, and list these across the top row of the grid.
3. Introduce the grid to students, and talk to them about the words and the features that are shown. Tell students that they are going to decide whether each word has any of the critical attributes that are listed across the top. If the word and attribute are related, they can place a plus sign in the box. If the words are not related, they can place a minus sign there. NOTE: This activity can be adapted for younger students by using a smiley face 😊 or an unhappy face ☹.

References

Johnson, D. D., and P. D. Pearson. 1984. *Teaching reading vocabulary*. New York: Holt, Rinehart and Winston.
Pittelman, S. D., J. E. Heimlich, R. L. Berglund, and M. P. French. 1991. *Semantic feature analysis: Classroom applications*. Newark, DE: International Reading Association.

SEMANTIC MAPS

When to Teach		Group Size		Grade Level	
Before Reading	📖	One-on-One	👥	PreK–2	🏫
During Reading		Small Group	👥	3–5	🏫
After Reading	📖	Whole Group	👥	6–8	🏫

R–Rationale

Semantic maps can be used to activate background knowledge about a topic (Heimlich and Pittelman 1986; Johnson and Pearson 1984). This strategy is similar to brainstorming using a web graphic. The difference between simple brainstorming and semantic mapping is that students take the initial topics and subtopics that are brainstormed and then arrange them in meaningful categories. As a result, semantic mapping encourages students to make determinations about relationships among the topics and subtopics. This type of strategy involves a more thoughtful process of analysis and reflection on the part of students.

E–Explanation

Semantic mapping is a visual illustration of how words are related to each other. It begins with a general brainstorming session, followed by the teacher and students working together to categorize the brainstormed words around shared relationships. This type of "process influences students to become active readers by triggering the brain to retrieve what is known about a topic and to use this information when reading" (Heimlich and Pittelman 1986, 3).

A–Application

The semantic map was created in Inspiration (http://www.inspiration.com), a software program that helps the user easily develop a semantic map. The teacher used the Rapid Fire feature of Inspiration during the brainstorming session. That feature enables the user to simply type in a word, select enter, and see the word immediately on the graphic organizer.

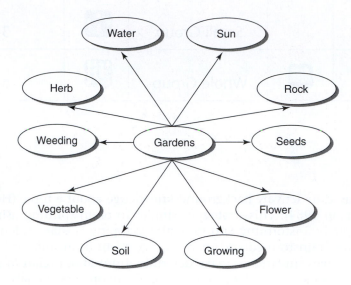

When the teacher and students finished brainstorming, they worked together to reorganize the diagram around central ideas or categories as shown below. It is simple to click and drag the circles in Inspiration and then add links to show the relationships among concepts.

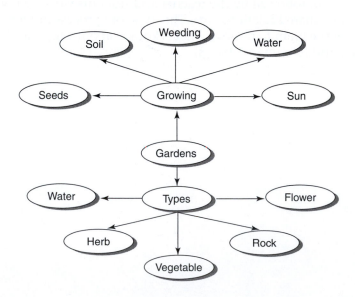

D–Delivery

Semantic mapping is a way to graphically represent key topics and concepts.

1. Select a word or topic, and list the word on the chalkboard, overhead, or projection screen.
2. Ask students to think of as many words as possible that relate to the word or topic, and list their answers on the semantic map.
3. Review the words listed on the map, and decide whether the words could be reorganized and grouped into categories. Help the students brainstorm these categories, and then work with them to organize the words into the categories.
4. If the word or topic is related to a theme of study, have students find new words to add to the map as the unit progresses. If the word or topic relates to a book, have them read the book and then add new words to the map based on their reading.

References

Heimlich, J. E., and S. D. Pittelman. 1986. *Semantic mapping: Classroom application*. Newark, DE: International Reading Association.

Johnson, D. D., and P. D. Pearson. 1984. *Teaching reading vocabulary*. New York: Holt, Rinehart and Winston.

VOCABULARY KNOWLEDGE RATING SCALE

When to Teach		Group Size		Grade Level	
Before Reading	📖	One-on-One	👥	PreK–2	
During Reading	📖	Small Group	👥	3–5	🏫
After Reading	📖	Whole Group	👥	6–8	🏫

R–Rationale

The vocabulary knowledge rating scale involves students in the exploration of vocabulary words they will encounter during the reading of a text. This type of strategy can help students actively look for and be aware of new vocabulary words. The reciprocal relationship between vocabulary and comprehension underscores how critical vocabulary is to the development of reading (Nagy and Anderson 1984; Stahl and Fairbanks 1986; Stanovich 2004). A child who encounters an unfamiliar word in print needs the vocabulary skills to be able to identify, or decode, the word as well as know how to determine the meaning of the word.

E–Explanation

The vocabulary knowledge rating scale is most effective when the teacher designates specific vocabulary words before students read and when students write those words in the first column of the chart. Introducing the words prior to students' reading heightens students' awareness of the new words they will encounter as they read. Students then note the page numbers where each word is located as they are reading. After reading, students work with a partner or small group to record the definitions as well as to look back in the text and write how the words were actually used in the story. If the word had multiple meanings, then students analyze how the word was used in the context of the story to decide the meaning that would be correct for the word.

A–Application

The teacher identifies vocabulary words from a story or other text that will be targeted during instruction and lists each word in the left column of the scale. Before reading, students note whether they are familiar with the word. If they have not seen or heard the word before, they note this with a ?; if they are familiar with the word, they mark it with a √. During reading, students note the page number of each word to refer back to later. After reading, students revisit the pages they noted and write the sentences that illustrate how the words were used in the text. They also look up each word in the dictionary to find a definition that matches how the word was used in the story.

Before Reading			During Reading	After Reading *Bloomability* by Sharon Creech
Vocabulary Word	*?*	*✓*	*Page # in Book*	*Write the definition, AND* *write how the word was used in the book.*
1. Jack-of-all-trades	?		1	**Definition:** *Noun—person who can do passable work at various tasks: a handy, versatile person.* **Example in text:** *He called himself a Jack-of-all-trades (Jack was his real name), but sometimes there wasn't any trade in whatever town we were living in, so off he would go in search of a job somewhere else.*

D–Delivery

The vocabulary knowledge rating scale focuses students' attention on specific vocabulary words they will read in a text.

1. Identify specific words that will be targeted in a story or other text.
2. Have students list the vocabulary words in the first column, or fill them in ahead of time.
3. Before they read the text, have students indicate in the appropriate column whether they are familiar with the word. If not, they place a question mark in that column. If they are familiar with the word, they place a check in that column.
4. As students read, have them note the page number of each vocabulary word to use later to refer back to the word.
5. After students have read the text, have them work with a partner or small group of three or four students to define the words and write how they were used in the text. Another option is to have students write each word in a new sentence that shows they understand how to use it correctly.
6. Meet with students in a large group to hear their findings about each vocabulary word and to ensure that there are no misconceptions about the words.

References

Nagy, W. E., and R. C. Anderson. 1984. How many words are there in printed English? *Reading Research Quarterly* 19: 304–30.

National Reading Panel. 2000. *Teaching children to read: An evidence-based assessment of the scientific research literature on reading and its implications for reading instruction* (NIH Publication No. 00-4769). Washington, DC: National Institute of Child Health and Human Development, National Institutes of Health.

Stahl, S. A., and M. M. Fairbanks. 1986. The effects of vocabulary instruction: A model-based meta-analysis. *Review of Educational Research* 56: 72–81.

Stanovich, K. E. 2004. Matthew effects in reading: Some consequences of individual differences in the acquisition of literacy. In *Theoretical models and processes of reading* (5th ed.), ed. R. B. Ruddell and N. J. Unrau, 454–516. Newark, DE: International Reading Association.

Vocabulary Knowledge Rating Scale

Name: _____   Date: _____

Book title: _____   Author: _____

Before Reading			During Reading	After Reading
Vocabulary Word	?	✓	Page # in Book	Write the definition, AND write how the word was used in the book.
1.				Definition: Example in text:
2.				Definition: Example in text:
3.				Definition: Example in text:
4.				Definition: Example in text:
5.				Definition: Example in text:

?   **I do no know this word.**

✓   **I am familiar with this word.**

VOCABULARY DOODLES

When to Teach		Group Size		Grade Level	
Before Reading		One-on-One	👥	PreK–2	🏫
During Reading		Small Group	👥	3–5	🏫
After Reading	📖	Whole Group	👥	6–8	🏫

R–Rationale

Vocabulary doodles involve students in exploring relationships among words. For a given vocabulary word, students identify clues or critical elements/attributes for the word along with an illustration. This type of activity builds on the notion of vocabulary illustrations, which Richardson and Morgan (2003) emphasize can enrich students' vocabulary knowledge.

E–Explanation

A simple scribble mark or doodle is the beginning point for an illustration of an assigned vocabulary word. Students supplement their illustrations with interesting information that relates to the vocabulary words they are studying. They present this information to see if others in the class can guess the word, based on the clues and the illustration.

A–Application

The teacher assigns a small group of students a vocabulary word—*symbiosis*, which means a long-term relationship between different kinds of organisms. He gives students the beginning doodle shown on the next page on the left. The illustration on the right shows how the students develop the doodle to represent a clown fish resting among sea anemones. At the bottom of the paper, students write down four clues that are related to their vocabulary word. They then present their illustration and clues to the rest of the class to see whether the class can identify their vocabulary word, which they have covered with a sticky note.

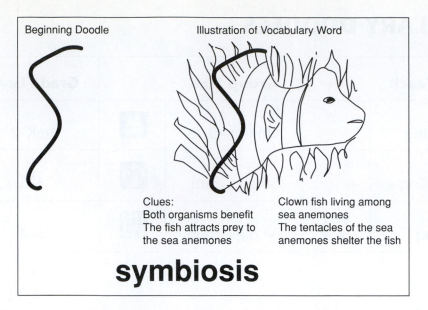

Beginning Doodle Illustration of Vocabulary Word

Clues:
Both organisms benefit
The fish attracts prey to
the sea anemones

Clown fish living among
sea anemones
The tentacles of the sea
anemones shelter the fish

symbiosis

D–Delivery

In vocabulary doodles, students create pictorial and/or graphical illustrations to represent a vocabulary word. They also identify key elements or attributes that describe or are associated with the word.

1. Draw a simple doodle starter on a large sheet of poster paper or manila paper.
2. Assign a vocabulary word to a small group of students.
3. Have students work with their group to research their word and identify four or five pieces of information about their vocabulary word.
4. Have students use the doodle to begin the illustration of their vocabulary word. The illustration should offer another clue regarding the vocabulary word.
5. Have students write the four to five items of information below the doodle.
6. Have students write the word at the bottom of the page but cover it with an index card or sticky note.
7. Have students present their work to the class, which tries to guess the word.

Reference

Richardson, J. S., and R. F. Morgan. 2003. *Reading to learn in the content areas*. 5th ed. Belmont, CA: Wadsworth/ Thomson Learning.

WORD SORTS

When to Teach		Group Size		Grade Level	
Before Reading		One-on-One	👥	PreK–2	🏫
During Reading		Small Group	👥	3–5	🏫
After Reading		Whole Group	👥	6–8	🏫

R–Rationale

Word sorts (Bear et al. 1996; Gillet and Temple 1978) is a strategy designed to help students see the generative nature of words. The strategy assists students in seeing patterns in words, identifying relationships among words, and categorizing words based on those relationships.

E–Explanation

Word sorts involve the manipulation or sorting of a set of words written on index cards or slips of paper into groups based on commonalities, relationships, related concepts, and/or other criteria. Word sorts typically consist of ten to twenty words, depending on the age of the students. It is important that the students completely understand the words because they are not able to identify patterns and relationships if they do not understand the meanings of the words. If possible, it is better to use words from the students. This can be accomplished by giving students a topic and having them brainstorm words, making sure that all students know and understand a word prior to adding it to the list.

There are two basic kinds of word sorts: open and closed. An open sort is more complex; it requires students to identify the patterns and relationships among the words and come up with their own categories. In a closed sort, the category is provided, and students simply identify commonalities in the words to fit the category. It is suggested that students work with closed sorts before moving to open sorts. It is also more beneficial to students when word sorts are done frequently for ten to fifteen minutes instead of occasionally for longer periods of time. Word sorts can be general, intended to help develop students' abilities to see patterns and relationships, or they can follow a reading selection, using specific words from the text.

A–Application

After the first grade class finished reading the story *The Cow That Went Oink* by Bernard Most, the students made the following list of farm animals: cow, horse, pig, alligator (yes, there are alligator farms), turkey, dog, hen, goose, cat, goat, sheep, and rooster. While the students worked in centers, the teacher wrote the words on index cards, making five sets. The students were then assigned to small groups and given a set of cards. The teacher explained that they were going to play a closed sorting game called Follow the Rule. He gave the students a rule/category, and in their groups they talked about the animals while sorting them to fit the given rule. For example, for the category of animals with four legs, the students sorted their cards into two groups: those that followed the rule (i.e., cow, horse, pig, alligator, dog, cat, goat, sheep) and those that did not (i.e., turkey, hen, goose, rooster).

The students continued sorting their cards according to the different categories provided by the teacher.

- Animals that can fly
- Animals with sharp teeth
- Animals with fur
- Animals with feathers
- Animal names that are one syllable
- Animal names that follow the short-vowel pattern

The students talked, decided on a category, and then sorted their animal cards into two groups: one group that fit their category and one group that did not. The teacher allowed the groups to move around to each other's groups and try to identify the relationships for the other groups' categories. After all the groups had a chance to rotate and check out the other groups, they all shared their categories.

D–Delivery

Students need guidance and modeling when first being introduced to word sorts, but with practice they become proficient at identifying patterns and relationships among words.

1. Select ten to twenty words that can be sorted and are based on the topic under study. These words can be generated by teacher and/or students, but all students must have a clear understanding of the words.
2. Copy the words on individual cards or slips of paper. Each student or group of students needs a set of words.
3. Decide whether you want to do an open or closed sort. If a closed sort, present categories for students to use as they sort. If an open sort, let students select their own categories for sorting the words.
4. Have students work in pairs or in small groups. Remind them that the rationale behind their sorting is more important than whether a word goes into a category or not.
5. Conduct a group discussion after each sort, and allow students to revise their categories, if desired.
6. If students do an open sort, have them label their categories with sticky notes so that you will recognize the thinking behind their sort. Ask students to share their categories with the class and explain their rationale for placing words in different categories.

References

Bear, D. R., M. Invernizzi, S. Templeton, and F. Johnston. 1996. *Words their way: Word study for phonics, vocabulary, and spelling instruction.* Upper Saddle River, NJ: Merrill/Prentice Hall.

Gillet, J. W., and C. Temple. 1978. Word knowledge: A cognitive view. *Reading World* 18: 132–40.

Most, Bernard. 1990. *The Cow That Went OINK.* New York: Harcourt.

Section VI

Comprehension

The United States federal legislation Reading First defines reading comprehension as the reading processes used to obtain meaning from print, media, or graphic communication. It also clearly states that comprehension is the main reason for reading (National Reading Panel 2000). There is often a misconception that students are comprehending what they read when they decode, or sound out, words. This is simply not true. A major goal of reading is for students to construct meaning, which is what comprehension is all about.

Research has shown that students can benefit from the explicit teaching of comprehension strategies (National Reading Panel 2000; Pressley and Wharton-McDonald 1997). Research has also shown that comprehension instruction does not receive enough time and attention in the primary and upper grades (Snow 2003). Our goal should be to help students be good readers who approach reading with a purpose, very clear about why they are reading a text and what they expect to get from the reading. Specifically, good readers do (Pressley and Wharton-McDonald 1997, 450–51):

- Actively look for information related to their goal.
- Activate prior knowledge and relate important points in the text to one another.
- Construct hypotheses and conclusions about what they are reading.
- Review and preview segments of text as they consciously integrate ideas encountered in different parts of the text.
- Fill information gaps in the text through inferencing.
- Monitor their reading.
- Feel passionate about their reading.

Good readers also need to develop their metacognitive skills. Metacognition is the ability to know when something being read does not make sense and a knowledge of strategies that can be used to fix the problem. Metacognition is knowing what we know, knowing what we are reading about, and knowing when something needs to be corrected. Proficient readers show evidence of metacognition every time they read. They know when to reread a piece of text, when to skip and read ahead, or where they need to go to find more information to construct meaning from a text. Struggling readers often lack a sense of metacognition; they do not have these monitoring strategies in place.

Students need explicit instruction in how to be metacognitive readers. When teachers take time to explicitly teach comprehension strategies, they are laying a foundation that builds students' metacognitive awareness. In order for the comprehension instruction to be effective, teachers have to learn how to interact with students at the right time and the right place during the reading of a text. Students also need multiple opportunities to apply comprehension skills and strategies with a variety of texts. All readers benefit from direct, explicit instruction that focuses on how and when to use comprehension strategies. It is the modeling provided by the teacher that helps make an abstract concept more concrete.

References

National Reading Panel. 2000. *Teaching children to read: An evidence-based assessment of the scientific research literature on reading and its implications for reading instruction* (NIH Publication No. 00-4769). Washington, DC: National Institute of Child Health and Human Development, National Institutes of Health.

Pressley, M., and R. Wharton-McDonald. 1997. Skilled comprehension and its development through instruction. *School Psychology Review* 26: 448–66.

Snow, C. 2003. Assessment of reading comprehension: Researchers and practitioners helping themselves and each other. In *Rethinking reading comprehension*, ed. A. Sweet and C. Snow, 254–69. New York: Guilford.

ANTICIPATION GUIDE

When to Teach		Group Size		Grade Level	
Before Reading	📖	One-on-One	👥	PreK–2	🏫
During Reading	📖	Small Group	👥	3–5	🏫
After Reading	📖	Whole Group	👥	6–8	🏫

R–Rationale

Anticipation guides (Readence, Bean, and Baldwin 1998) inspire lively discussions about the topic to be read or studied, thus increasing motivation and desire to read the selection while fostering prior knowledge. This strategy also helps students set a purpose for reading and encourages higher-order thinking skills.

E–Explanation

An anticipation guide is a strategy designed to activate and/or build prior knowledge and to challenge students' preconceived notions about the text to be read. A guide consists of statements that the students respond to before they read. The statements are usually true or false statements, which are supported by the students through class discussion. It is important that these are broad statements and not specific details that are easily known as right or wrong. After reading the selection, students should return to the anticipation guide and determine whether they still agree with their original responses. Some teachers also allow students to return to the guide and make adjustments during their reading.

A–Application

Prior to a text selection about volcanoes, the teacher develops an anticipation guide to activate students' schema about the topic, to initiate interest in reading the selection, and to informally assess their prior knowledge about the content to be studied. The guide includes four broad statements related to volcanoes. The teacher distributes the guides to the students and allows them a few minutes to react to the statements by agreeing or disagreeing with them. The teacher then involves students in a brief class discussion, encouraging them to share the reasoning behind their reactions. She then gives students an opportunity to change their responses, if desired. Next, the students read the selection and then return to their anticipation guides to confirm and/or disconfirm their original predictions. The teacher guides the students in sharing their revised thoughts and encourages students to return to the text to provide evidence for their decisions.

Before Reading T or F	Statements	After Reading T or F
F	1. A dormant volcano is no threat to people living in the surrounding area.	T
F	2. More than 80% of the earth's surface has come from volcanoes.	T
T	3. One of the most devastating volcanic eruptions was Mt. St. Helens in southwest Washington State in 1980.	T
T	4. Magma is a heavy substance that sinks to the bottom of a volcano.	F

D–Delivery

Anticipation guides not only prepare students for reading but also help to form connections between the students and the text. Students are able to pull from their mental filing cabinets to answer the statements on the guides. Anticipation guides also set a purpose for reading and encourage higher-order thinking skills.

1. After choosing the text that students will read, analyze the text for critical ideas, information, and issues.
2. Determine key ideas about which students may have background knowledge and information or issues about which students might have misinformation.
3. Write several (usually three to eight) statements that will precipitate discussion around all of the key points. Do not make the statements dependent on reading the passage; rather, create statements around which students can state their opinions without having read the text. The statements should tap into students' background knowledge. Leave space next to the statements for students to respond—individually, in small groups, or in the whole group.
4. Introduce the topic to students, and give them the following directions:
   • Read each of the key ideas, and note whether you agree or disagree with the statement.
   • (optional) Work with a partner or small group to discuss each of the key ideas, comparing and contrasting your responses to the statements. Make a group decision regarding agreement or disagreement.
   • Read the assigned text.
   • Revisit the anticipation guide to determine whether you have changed your mind as a result of reading the selection. Locate sections in the text that support your newfound knowledge.
   • (optional) Provide the page numbers where you found justification for your responses.
5. Use students' responses to the statements in the anticipation guide as the foundation for discussion and/or as a way for students to develop questions for further reading, inquiry, and/or research.

Reference

Readence, J., T. Bean, and R. Baldwin. 1998. *Content area reading: An integrated approach.* 6th ed. Dubuque, IA: Kendall Hunt.

CHARACTER ANALYSIS

When to Teach		Group Size		Grade Level	
Before Reading		One-on-One		PreK–2	
During Reading		Small Group		3–5	
After Reading		Whole Group		6–8	

R–Rationale

Characters help students move into and through text and also affect what readers come away with from the text (Martinez and Roser 2005). The character analysis strategy teaches students to examine the way a character talks, interacts with people, dresses, and acts in order to learn about a character's personality. Students' understanding of the characterization they encounter in text will transfer to their own stories. "Classrooms where teachers and students take time to read and discuss authentic literature" will be ones in which the students "both understand and craft increasingly rich characterizations of their own" (Graves 2005, 3).

E–Explanation

Character analysis is a way for students to explore a story to see how the author created a particular character. Characters are at the heart of a good story; they can make us laugh, cry, and feel for them through the way the author uses them to tell the story. Characters are what make us love a story, and they are a major part of what draws us back to a story to keep reading. A character's actions and interactions can tell readers a lot about that character.

The character analysis strategy asks students to select a specific character to study. They first brainstorm traits that describe this character, such as loyal, courageous, cowardly, or persistent. For each trait that is identified, students must provide evidence from the story to support the trait. For example, if the trait is loyalty, what does the character do or say in the story that shows he or she is loyal? In the evidence section, students are asked to provide a summary and also note the page number in the book where they found this evidence. Once students have finished the character analysis, they discuss as a class or in small groups what they found for each character. This type of character analysis provides a bridge to writing when students need help developing characters in their own stories.

A–Application

The teacher identifies a key stopping point for character analysis in the book *A Wrinkle in Time* by Madeline L'Engle. He encourages the students to stop their reading on page 2 and reread:

> *And on the way home from school, walking up the road with her arms full of books, one of the boys had said something about her "dumb baby brother." At this she'd thrown the books on the side of the road and tackled him with every ounce of strength she had, and arrived home with her blouse torn and a big bruise under one eye.*

After rereading, the teacher has students turn and talk with their partners about Meg's actions. Those discussions are then brought to the whole group as the class contributes these ideas about Meg:

- She will not hesitate to stand up for her brother.
- She loves her brother, Charles Wallace.
- She will do what it takes to protect him from people who do not understand him.

The students then use this analysis of Meg to arrive at the character trait that she is protective of her brother, and the evidence is a summary of this part of the book, in which she fought a boy who criticized her brother.

D–Delivery

Students select a character to analyze and then identify characteristics that describe that character. They use examples from the book to provide evidence for each characteristic.

1. Using a story the class is reading, brainstorm with students examples of possible traits for a specific character in the story.
2. Select one of the traits, and record it on the character analysis chart.
3. Ask students what they have read in the story that supports this particular trait. If necessary, have them refer to a specific place in the text to verify.
4. Record the example from the book in the part of the box marked Evidence.
5. Break students into smaller groups of three to four, and assign each group a trait from the list that was brainstormed earlier. Ask them to work together to find evidence to support the trait.
6. Bring the class back together, and ask each group to present its trait and the evidence to support that trait. As each group presents, have students record the findings on their character analysis charts.

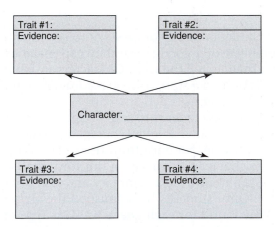

References

Graves, D. H. 2005. The centrality of character. In *What a character! Character study as a guide to literary meaning making in grades K–8*, ed. N. L. Roser and M. G. Martinez, 3–5. Newark, DE: International Reading Association.

Martinez, M. G., and N. L. Roser 2005. Students' developing understanding of character. In *What a character! Character study as a guide to literary meaning making in grades K–8*, ed. N. L. Roser and M. G. Martinez, 6–12. Newark, DE: International Reading Association.

CUBING

When to Teach		Group Size		Grade Level	
Before Reading		One-on-One	👥	PreK–2	
During Reading		Small Group	👥	3–5	🏫
After Reading	📖	Whole Group	👥	6–8	🏫

R–Rationale

Cubing (Cowan and Cowan 1980) encourages students to view a topic from various perspectives and to use their speaking and/or writing skills to demonstrate their understanding. This strategy not only increases students' understanding of the topic but also strengthens their higher-order thinking skills.

E–Explanation

Cubing is an after-reading comprehension strategy that pushes students to explore a topic from multiple perspectives, requiring varying levels of thinking. The strategy is called cubing because a cube has six sides and the strategy requires students to view the topic under study from six perspectives: describe it, compare it, associate it, analyze it, apply it, and argue for or against it. These six perspectives provide a springboard for writing about or discussing the topic being studied.

A–Application

The students in a fifth-grade classroom have just finished reading a selection about the life cycle of a butterfly. Following the reading assignment, the teacher divides the class into six groups. Each group is given several sheets of paper to use in its completion of the assigned task. The teacher then has each group select a number from one to six. After the numbers have been selected, the teacher produces a cube with each of the six sides numbered and labeled with a different thinking task. She provides each group with the corresponding perspective from which the students are to review and consider the information just read. The groups discuss the life cycle of the butterfly from the assigned perspective and then prepare a brief report to share with the class. One group describes the life cycle; another compares it to something that has been previously studied; a third group associates it with something they already know and understand; another group analyzes it by breaking it down into specific parts; a fifth group applies the information in a creative way; and the last group takes a stand for or against it. Each group shares its perspective with the rest of the class, thereby providing a thorough investigation of the life cycle of a butterfly.

D–Delivery

Cubing allows students to use varying levels of thinking to explore a topic from multiple perspectives.

1. Introduce the topic. This might include a lecture, reading a selection, and so on.
2. Present a six-sided cube, or have students think of one, with sides labeled Describe it, Compare it, Associate it, Analyze it, Apply it, and Argue for or against it.
3. Assign the students a perspective to consider, or allow each student to consider all six sides of the cube. You can also form groups of six, and have each member of the group consider and respond to one side of the cube, before sharing with the rest of the group. Or you can form six groups, give each group a different perspective to consider, and then have each group share with the rest of the students.
4. Give students five minutes to consider the assigned perspective(s).
5. Ask them to talk or write about the topic from the assigned perspective(s).

Reference

Cowan, G., and E. Cowan. 1980. *Writing*. New York: Wiley.

DIRECTED READING AND THINKING ACTIVITY

When to Teach		Group Size		Grade Level	
Before Reading	📖	One-on-One	👥	PreK–2	🏫
During Reading	📖	Small Group	👥	3–5	🏫
After Reading	📖	Whole Group	👥	6–8	🏫

R–Rationale

The directed reading and thinking activity (DR–TA) is a way to guide students through the comprehension process, teaching them how to draw on their background knowledge as they make predictions about the text (Stauffer 1969). This strategy helps students learn how to talk about what is going on in their heads, which can often help them work through a misunderstanding as they move through the process. Good readers tend to do this already; it is struggling readers who will benefit from this type of lesson.

E–Explanation

The DR–TA is a teaching strategy that involves cycles of making predictions, reading the text, revising predictions based on what has been read, and then repeating the process. It is designed to support students' comprehension by showing them how to monitor their understanding. The goal is for the teacher to move away from asking just yes or no questions. Instead, the teacher should ask students to share what they think is going to happen and also why they think this will happen. Although the DR–TA is teacher led, the ultimate goal is for students to internalize the process of monitoring their comprehension by continuously thinking about what they are reading.

A–Application

When preparing the DR–TA lesson, the teacher previews the story to determine stopping points where students can pause and ponder what is happening in the story. As the students read, the teacher stops them at each of those points and encourages students to mentally confirm or disconfirm their initial thoughts about the text. The teacher also guides the students to share the reasoning behind their thoughts. The students then continue reading to test their revised or new theory until the next stopping point.

D–Delivery

The DR–TA begins with open-ended, divergent questions, which gradually become more focused as students acquire more information from the text. The teacher should encourage students to continuously process what they are reading and to draw on new text-based information as they progress through the story.

1. Prior to their reading of the story, ask students to consider these questions:
   - What do you think the story will be about?
   - What makes you think so?
2. As they read each segment of the text, have students consider these questions:
   - Based on what you have read so far, would you change your prediction? Why or why not?
   - What happened in the story that makes you think your prediction is or is not correct?
   - Do you have any new predictions you would like to make?
   - What do you think will happen next?
   - What did you read that makes you think this might happen?
   - How do you think this story will end? Why do you think so?
3. After they have read the story, ask students to consider these questions:
   - When did you know how the story was going to end?
   - How did you know this?
   - What do you think about how the story ended?
   - Did this make sense to you?

Reference

Stauffer, R. G. 1969. *Directing reading maturity as a cognitive process*. New York: Harper & Row.

DISCUSSION WEB

When to Teach		Group Size		Grade Level	
Before Reading		One-on-One		PreK–2	🏫
During Reading		Small Group	👥	3–5	🏫
After Reading	📖	Whole Group	👥	6–8	🏫

R–Rationale

Discussion webs (Alvermann 1991) are designed to include all students in active participation in class discussions. This strategy helps develop students' cooperative learning skills. It also helps students develop a mental framework for looking at two sides of an issue and for processing opposing and/or supporting evidence before taking a stand.

E–Explanation

The discussion web incorporates reading, writing, speaking, and listening as students explore two sides of an issue. Teachers recognize the importance of classroom discussions in developing students' thinking but often find it difficult to involve the entire class in the discussions. Sometimes students are reluctant to participate, and only a few students actually contribute to the conversation. Discussion webs help involve all students as active participants in class discussions.

A–Application

After reading the book *Encounter* by Jan Brett, students work in pairs to explore this question: Was the discovery of the New World a good thing? The teacher provides each pair of students with a blank discussion web on which they record their pros and cons by writing key words in the Yes or No columns. The teacher encourages the students to come up with an equal number of pros and cons, if possible, supporting their answers with evidence from their reading. After discussion, each pair of students draws a conclusion and writes its rationale at the bottom of the web. The teacher then combines each pair with another set of partners and directs these four-student groups to compare their responses and conclusions before completing a new discussion web. Each new group of four works to reach a consensus on its response to the central question and then chooses a spokesperson to share its position with the class. The teacher allows three minutes for each group to share its position and reasoning. After whole-group discussion, each student writes a personal response to the question, providing rationale in support of that response.

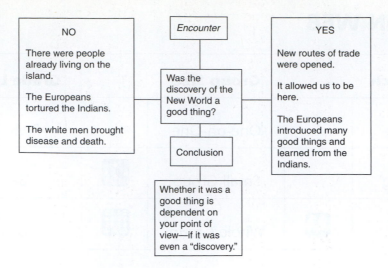

D–Delivery

Discussion webs are useful for discussions in almost all subject areas.

1. Choose a selection for student reading that is open to interpretation and possible opposing viewpoints. Prepare students for reading by activating relevant background knowledge, and establish a purpose for reading.
2. After students read the selection, introduce the discussion web, and provide a focus question for discussion.
3. Assign students to work with a partner or in small groups to develop opposing sides of the question. Encourage students to throw the evidence on the table and to hash things out among themselves. Remind students to return to the text as needed for evidence to support their opinions. When this strategy is first introduced, model this thinking and talking process for the students.
4. After students share viewpoints and complete the discussion web, group each set of students with another group. Have the new groups share their thoughts and work on reaching a consensus response to the question. Have them add additional arguments to the discussion web and/or complete another web. The new group's final conclusion is written at the bottom of the web.
5. Have the combined groups share with the entire group. Give each spokesperson a time limit, usually two to three minutes. Such a limit reduces the likelihood that the last group will have nothing to add to the discussion.
6. Have students write their own personal responses to the focus question. The discussion web provides them with a framework for getting out their thoughts about the question while allowing them to reflect on the contributions of their classmates.

Reference

Alvermann, D. 1991. The discussion web: A graphic aid for learning across the curriculum. *The Reading Teacher* 45: 92–99.

GO! CHART

When to Teach		Group Size		Grade Level	
Before Reading	📖	One-on-One		PreK–2	🏫
During Reading	📖	Small Group	👥	3–5	🏫
After Reading	📖	Whole Group	👥	6–8	🏫

R–Rationale

The GO! Chart (Benson and Cummins 2000) is designed to help students dig deeper into a story in order to reach higher levels of understanding. It also helps them see the metacognitive processes readers experience before/during/after reading.

E–Explanation

A GO! Chart is a hierarchical graphic organizer that engages students' thinking at progressively higher levels before, during, and after reading. The teacher guides the class through oral discussions designed to activate and build topic knowledge prior to reading; identify content-related vocabulary words; share understandings of the text; encourage wonderings that go beyond the text; help students make connections with the content; and organize final thoughts about the story. The GO! Chart may take several days to complete, depending on the complexity of the text and the depth of the discussion. Generally, teachers take about four days to complete the chart categories.

A–Application

The teacher draws a blank GO! Chart on a large piece of bulletin board paper and introduces the story *The Day of Ahmed's Secret* (Heide Gilliland 1995) to the class. The students use clues from the title and the cover to make predictions about what the text might be about, while the teacher records their predictions in the first column of the chart. With each prediction, the teacher prompts the students to share their thinking and rationale for the prediction. Students continue giving predictions, with the teacher providing additional clues as needed (e.g., a picture walk, reading sections of the text aloud, and so on). The teacher then reviews the predictions, which students use to predict words the author might use in the story. As students provide the words, they connect each to a prediction and provide a rationale for their thinking. The students then read the story. Thereafter, the class revisits the story and vocabulary predictions in order to confirm or disconfirm each contribution. The teacher then guides the students in completing the next three columns: Understandings, which help students share things they noticed while reading; Interpretations, which extend their thinking about things not explicitly stated in the story; and Connections, which help students make a personal connection to what has been read. Students then use a shape map to organize their thoughts about the beginning, middle, and end of the story.

The Day of Ahmed's Secret					
Predictions	Vocabulary	Understandings	Interpretations	Connections	Organizers
I think this book might be about . . . • a surprise birthday party • a boy that did something wrong • a family that is getting a new baby • aliens that are coming to blow up the earth • traveling to a strange place	*I think the author might use the word . . .* party happy sad fun space ship *I know the author will use the word . . .* butagaz rosewater	*I noticed . . .* • the boy worked hard • Ahmed had a cart • Ahmed liked where he lived • there are pyramids in Cairo	*I wonder . . .* • why Ahmed wasn't in school • why Ahmed's dad didn't work • how Ahmed learned to write his name	*This reminds me of . . .* • the day I told Mema about learning to ride my bike • when we read a book about Egypt • the movie the Mummy	Cairo Ahmed Ahmed had to finish his chores before sharing his secret * Ahmed visited with friends * delivered fuel * ate lunch Ahmed went home and shared his secret with his family

D–Delivery

The GO! Chart is created on a long piece of bulletin board paper divided into six columns: Predictions, Vocabulary, Understandings, Interpretations, Connections, and Organizers. The chart should remain whole during the entire daily or weekly lesson; it not only helps students dig deeper into the content but also helps them see the thinking that good readers do before, during, and after reading. With modifications the GO! Chart can also be used with nonfiction.

1. Use Column 1 to help activate and/or establish schema by guiding students in making predictions about the story in response to a variety of clues provided by the author.
   a. Introduce the story, and have students make predictions about it, using the title, cover, illustrations, and so on.
   b. Write student predictions on the chart, making sure that students provide rationales for their thoughts. Use open-ended prompts such as, "What makes you say that?" "Tell me more," or "Share your thoughts."
2. Use Column 2 to extend the plot predictions as you encourage students to predict words that the author might use in order to develop the story as predicted.
   a. As students predict vocabulary words that might be in the story, chart their responses. Make sure that students can connect the words they provide with a prediction in Column 1.
   b. If needed, introduce any uncommon words found in the story, and include them on the chart.
3. Have students read the story (orally or silently) or listen to it as you read it aloud.
4. Have students return to Columns 1 and 2 to confirm or disconfirm their plot and vocabulary predictions.
5. Use Columns 3–5 to help students explore their comprehension of the story on a variety of levels: knowledge recall, analysis and interpretation, and evaluation. Guide the discussion of the story as students share their responses to the following prompts:
   a. Understandings: "I noticed . . ."
   b. Wonderings: "I wonder . . ."
   c. Connections: "This reminds me of . . ."

6. Use the final column to develop a graphic organizer to help organize the story (i.e., shape map, concept map, hierarchical map, Venn diagram).
   a. Have students revisit the facts identified in the Understandings column, discuss their purpose in organizing the facts (e.g., retelling, identifying key facts, recreating the story plot), and then select the most appropriate graphic organizer to use in organizing the information.
   b. Work with students to complete the chosen graphic organizer.

References

Benson, V., and C. Cummins. 2000. *The power of retelling: Developmental steps for building comprehension.* Bothell, WA: Wright Group/McGraw-Hill.

Heide, F. 1995. *The Day of Ahmed's Secret.* New York: HarperTrophy.

GO! Chart

Predictions	Vocabulary	Understandings	Interpretations	Connections	Organizers
I think this book might be about . . .	*I think the author might use the word . . .* *I know the author will use the word . . .*	*I noticed . . .*	*I wonder . . .*	*This reminds me of . . .*	

K-W-L

When to Teach		Group Size		Grade Level	
Before Reading	📖	One-on-One		PreK–2	🏫
During Reading		Small Group	👥	3–5	🏫
After Reading	📖	Whole Group	👥	6–8	🏫

R–Rationale

The K-W-L (Ogle 1986) is designed to help the reader activate prior knowledge of a topic, set a purpose for reading the text, and become more focused in reading the text. This strategy also helps the teacher assess what students already know and what needs to be taught to help students learn the content being studied.

E–Explanation

K-W-L is an instructional activity to assist students in developing a framework and to actively engage them in constructing meaning from text. The basic instructional activity consists of three parts: First, readers identify what is KNOWN about a topic. Second, readers identify what they WANT to know about the topic. Finally, readers identify what was LEARNED from reading the text. Many modifications/additions to the K-W-L strategy can be made, depending on the additional information requested by the teacher. K-W-L Plus adds research and resources to the chart; K-W-L-Q adds questions that the students still have about the topic.

A–Application

The teacher prepares the K-W-L chart for a unit on frogs by drawing three columns and labeling each with a letter—K, W, and L. The teacher then guides the discussion as students respond to the prompts identified by the letters and he records their responses on the chart. He begins by asking students what they know about frogs. Students share their responses, and the teacher writes them on the chart in the column labeled K. Students then review what they think they know about frogs in order to generate questions they hope will be answered in the upcoming unit. The teacher enters these questions in the W column. After the unit is completed, students return to the chart and record their new information in the L column. Students also revisit the K and W columns to determine whether their questions were answered and whether their initial thoughts about the topic were accurate.

	Frogs	
K	**W**	**L**
Frogs are amphibians. Frogs were tadpoles when they were little. Frogs give people warts. Frogs eat flies.	Do frogs really give people warts? How many different types of frogs are there? Are all frogs green?	Frogs come in numerous sizes and colors. There are hundreds of different kinds of frogs. Frogs have long, sticky tongues.

D–Delivery

The teacher can create a class K-W-L graphic organizer chart or can make individual copies for students to use. The teacher introduces the topic and writes it at the top of the chart. Then teacher and students collaboratively complete the chart.

1. Give the first prompt: "What do you know about _____?" Write students' responses on the chart during the open discussion.
2. (optional) Ask students to find ideas that go together. Develop headings/categories that describe the ideas, and place these headings/categories at the bottom of the K column.
3. Have students respond to the second prompt: "What do you want to know about _____?" Write their responses on the chart. Any headings/categories developed previously may help students generate questions about what they would like to know.
4. Teach the lesson or have students read the selection.
5. Have students respond to the final prompt: "What did you learn about _____?" If students identify new categories of information they learned, write these ideas on the bottom of the column.
6. Have students revisit the first two columns to make any necessary changes in their prereading knowledge and/or to determine whether their questions were answered. Unanswered questions open the door for additional research.

Reference

Ogle, D. 1986. K-W-L: A teaching model that develops active reading of expository text. *Journal of Reading* 30: 626–31.

PLOT GRAPH

When to Teach		Group Size		Grade Level	
Before Reading	📖	One-on-One	👥	PreK–2	🏫
During Reading	📖	Small Group	👥	3–5	🏫
After Reading	📖	Whole Group	👥	6–8	🏫

R–Rationale

A plot graph gives students a way to visually represent these key elements of a story: the actions that lead the reader to the problem, the rising action, and the resolution to the story. This strategy requires students to be able to recognize key events in a story and then analyze each event, assigning it a positive or negative value.

E–Explanation

The plot of a story is usually the major focus of how the story is told. It involves a problem or conflict that is developed through the events in the story, with a resolution to the problem occurring by the end of the story. The plot is basically a series of actions that move in a logical sequence (i.e., beginning, middle, end) to a final outcome. A plot graph is an excellent way to help students illustrate the events in a story as they discuss the plot. A plot graph shows two quadrants of a graph, with the upper quadrant being positive and the lower quadrant being negative. Major story events are plotted on the graph chronologically to help students see the rising action that occurs in the story. This strategy is adapted from the positive and negative graph in Linda Rief's *Seeking Diversity* (1992).

A–Application

After reading the story *Summer of the Sea Serpent* by Mary Pope Osborne, the class identifies ten key events in the story: two from the beginning, six from the middle, and two from the end. The class assigns each event a rating from −4 to +4 as the teacher writes the event on the plot graph. The teacher then connects all the points to provide a visual interpretation of the key events in the story. The students use the graph to see the rising action of the climax of the story.

Example of a Plot Map

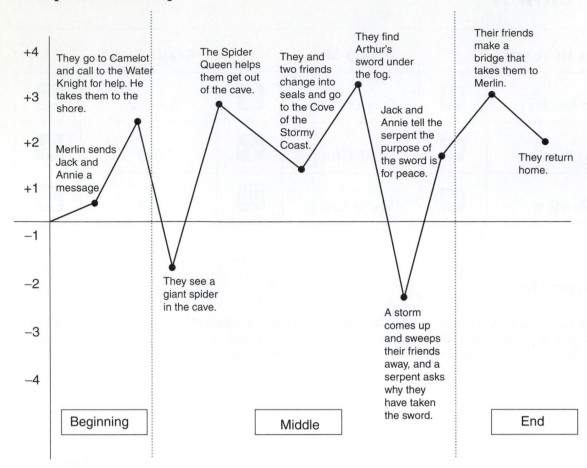

D–Delivery

A plot graph is a way to visually represent the events in a story.

1. Develop a graph that shows the two quadrants on the right side, with the upper quadrant being positive and the lower quadrant being negative.
2. Add a rating scale to the vertical axis to identify positive and negative events.
3. Have students identify key events in the story. These should reflect an awareness of the problem, the rising action, and the climax of the story.
4. Have students take each major event they have identified and plot it on the graph, using the positive and negative values of the rating scale to show event impact in the overall plot.
5. Have students identify/label those events that fall in the beginning, the middle, and the end of the story.
6. Encourage students to add symbols or other graphics to represent key events included on the plot graph.
7. As an extension to this activity, have students use the plot map to write a summary of the story in a narrative format.

References

Osborne, M. P. 2004. *Summer of the sea serpent*. New York: Random House.
Rief, L. 1992. *Seeking diversity: Language arts with adolescents*. Portsmouth, NH: Heinemann.

QUESTION–ANSWER RELATIONSHIPS

When to Teach		Group Size		Grade Level	
Before Reading		One-on-One	👥	PreK–2	
During Reading		Small Group	👥	3–5	🏫
After Reading	📖	Whole Group	👥	6–8	🏫

R–Rationale

Question–answer relationships (QAR; Raphael 1982) encourage students to analyze the task demands of questions prior to answering them. This strategy helps students categorize comprehension questions according to where students are likely to find the answers in the text: text explicit (i.e., the answer can be found directly in the text), text implicit (i.e., the answer must be derived from several locations in the text), and script implicit (i.e., the answer requires combining information from the text with personal experiences).

E–Explanation

QAR is an approach to questioning that enhances students' ability to answer comprehension questions by giving them a way to analyze the task demands of different question probes. QAR highlights four types of questions: right-there, think-and-search, author-and-you, and on-your-own (Raphael 1982). These should be initially introduced one at a time, and students should be given multiple opportunities to practice locating answers at that level before a new question type is introduced. It is also important that questions be used in conjunction with text as shown on next page.

A–Application

This teacher is just beginning to use the QAR strategy with her third-grade class, so she plans a lesson to focus on right-there questions. To prepare for the selection to be read, the teacher generates several questions whose answers are explicitly stated in the text. She has the students read the selection, and then she presents the list of questions to be answered. She reads the first question and uses the think-aloud approach to model how to locate the answer in the text. She locates the answer, reads the section containing the answer aloud, and spotlights the answer by covering it with transparent colored removable tape. The students then work in pairs to locate the remaining answers. Once all questions are answered, volunteers read the questions and show where the answers are located in the text. To extend their learning, the teacher has the students work in small groups to generate additional questions that are right-there. The students write their questions on the overhead, and the class collaboratively locates and shares the answers.

In-the-Book Questions	In-My-Head Questions
Right-There Questions	**Author-and-You Questions**
This type of question is sometimes called literal because the answer is usually found within a single sentence. The words used to ask the question and the words used to answer the question are *right there* in the text.	Readers have to draw on their own knowledge to answer these questions, while also thinking about what the author tells them.
Think-and-Search Questions	**On-My-Own Questions**
These answers can be found by looking in several sentences in the text. They might involve an explanation, comparing/contrasting, identifying cause/effect, or examples.	These answers are not found in the text. In most cases, readers draw on their own experiences and can answer the questions without reading the text.

D–Delivery

In order for students to fully utilize the QAR strategy, they must have time to develop an understanding of the four types of questions involved in the strategy. Therefore, the first few steps of this procedure are not intended to be implemented in one lesson but over several lessons. Begin by teaching the two major categories with related types of questions.

1. In the book.
   a. Right-there questions can be answered directly from the text. These questions often feature extended phrases from the text. For example, a question that reads, "Who traveled from Spain to discover the new world?" would be a right-there question because a sentence in the text reads, "Christopher Columbus traveled from Spain and discovered the new world." Take students back into the text, and show them where these answers are found.
   b. Think-and-search questions are generally found in the text in more than one sentence. The previous question becomes a think-and-search question when the answer requires combined information from at least two sentences. For example, the sentence "Christopher Columbus embarked on his journey from Spain" is followed later with "Christopher Columbus discovered the new world in 1492."

2. In my head.
    a. Author-and-you questions require readers to play a role in formulating the answers. That is, readers must synthesize information from the text and their own evaluation. This does not mean that there is no correct answer but rather that the answer must be supported by logic from the text as well as from the reader.
    b. On-your-own questions ask the reader to formulate an opinion. In theory readers might not even need to read the text if they possess enough background knowledge about the topic. For example, "Do you believe that Christopher Columbus received the recognition he deserved for discovering the new world?"
3. Identify short text passages and questions to use in teaching QAR. If applicable, use the text generator software that accompanies the textbook to generate questions that match the question type being taught. This allows students to learn the QAR strategy while also learning the content being studied.
4. Prepare copies of the passages and the questions for students.
5. Introduce a question and the type, and explain how the answer can be located. Model for the students how to locate the answer by thinking out loud through this process.
6. After several modeled examples, invite students to take the lead in identifying and locating answers to questions.
7. Once all types of questions have been introduced to the students, have them use the strategy on their own to answer questions. To maintain proficiency with the strategy, occasionally have students share how they derived their answers to text questions.

Reference

Raphael, T. E. 1982. Teaching children question-answering strategies. *The Reading Teacher* 36: 186–91.

QUESTIONING THE AUTHOR

When to Teach		Group Size		Grade Level	
Before Reading		One-on-One	👥	PreK–2	
During Reading	📖	Small Group	👥	3–5	🏫
After Reading		Whole Group	👥	6–8	🏫

R–Rationale

Questioning the Author (QtA; Beck, McKeown, Hamilton and Kucan 1997) enhances student engagement with text by pulling students into the text as active learners instead of as passive extractors of textual information. This strategy assists students in building understanding of text through queries and discussion and helps make them aware of the need to pay attention to all of the text and text features in order to develop a fuller understanding of what the author is trying to convey.

E–Explanation

QtA is a framework for getting students to actively respond to text through (1) collaborative discussion, (2) utilization of strategies proficient readers use when engaged with text, and (3) promoting a more active search for meaning while reading. The strategy basically involves three major parts: planning, discussion, and implementation. Planning includes identifying the major ideas of the text and the questions and strategies needed to help obtain those ideas. Planning also includes the identification of potential problems that might be encountered while trying to acquire meaning during reading. In the beginning the teacher should segment the text where major ideas and/or problems might occur and develop queries to help students acquire the main ideas or avoid the pitfalls. The discussion phrase is designed to help students construct understanding of the ideas or concepts they have encountered in the text. Students present the ideas they have gotten from the text and then engage in a shared inquiry into meaning. The teacher does not dominate this conversation but collaborates with students, guiding them to an understanding of the author's ideas. The queries developed in the planning stage can facilitate this process. Implementation involves the actual execution of the strategy. Students are introduced to the notion of author fallibility and the realization that sometimes authors do not clearly get their ideas across to the reader. However, the QtA strategy can help students make sense of what the author is trying to convey. The teacher then models and explains the procedure for implementation.

A–Application

A teacher is planning to use QtA for a selection about manatees and dugongs. He reads the selection and concludes that the main understanding the reader should gain from the text is the fact that manatees and dugongs are in danger of becoming extinct. He believes this was the author's intent because the text contains multiple references to the problems the animals have in securing food, staying out of the way of boats, and so on. However, many of these references are not explicitly stated but are found in various access features (or text features as they are sometimes called) and other subtle places. The teacher marks these places in the text with sticky notes and writes queries or prompts to use in initiating a conversation about the text at these stopping points. As the students read the selection, the teacher stops them at each segment, points out some of the implicit information provided by the author, and prompts a discussion to lead the students into recognizing that the information is all connected to the concept of manatees and dugongs being endangered.

D–Delivery

QtA provides an engaging and thought-provoking way to have students work their way through a text. However, it is important that teachers are cautious in implementing the strategy so that students fully understand it. During the initial stages of implementation, teachers should model the process of identifying key ideas and developing queries so that students understand what good readers do as they read. Then as students become comfortable with the process, they should be encouraged to generate their own queries for a section of the material, also using sticky notes to identify problem areas where readers should stop and ponder. Students can work in pairs to guide each other in this process of questioning the author during reading.

1. Preview the reading selection, and decide what is most important for students to understand from the material. Identify any segments of the text that might create difficulties for students. Choose stopping points in the text at which to initiate discussion to clarify key ideas.
2. As students read the text, intervene at selected points, or segments, and pose queries, or probes, to initiate discussion. Preplanning these queries is important so that the discussion is not delayed and occurs at the most appropriate time.
3. Engage students in a discussion prompted by the queries. Encourage students to return to the text as needed to gather information to aid in the discussion. Do not dominate the conversation, but simply guide the discussion as needed.
4. Continue the process until the entire text has been read and understood.

Reference

Beck, I. L., M. G. McKeown, R. L. Hamilton, and L. Kucan. 1997. *Questioning the author: An approach for enhancing student engagement with text.* Newark, DE: International Reading Association.

RECIPROCAL TEACHING

When to Teach		Group Size		Grade Level	
Before Reading		One-on-One	👥	PreK–2	
During Reading	📖	Small Group	👥	3–5	🏫
After Reading		Whole Group	👥	6–8	🏫

R–Rationale

Reciprocal teaching (Palinscar and Brown 1986) is a comprehension strategy that helps students focus and monitor their reading in order to achieve high levels of understanding. This strategy helps students develop skills in four important comprehension processes: predicting, questioning, clarifying, and summarizing.

E–Explanation

Reciprocal teaching is a scaffolded discussion strategy that is built on four processes that proficient readers use to make meaning from text. It is an interactive dialogue between teacher and students regarding specific segments of a text. The teacher models and explains each of the four processes and the role each plays in comprehension. Predicting helps students to anticipate and speculate about what will be discussed in the text; questioning requires students to generate and ask questions about the passage; clarifying helps students focus on what makes the selection difficult to understand; and summarizing requires students to restate what they have read in their own words. Time to practice each of the processes is essential to help students understand the reciprocal teaching strategy. Once students understand each specific process, they are able to use them all collectively as they read.

A–Application

The teacher reviews with the class the four processes involved in reciprocal teaching. She then divides the class into groups of four and tells each group to determine who will fulfill each role—predictor, questioner, clarifier, and summarizer. Next, the teacher distributes the material on manatees to be read and points out the markings that identify where the students are to stop and discuss the reading. The students read the selection about manatees, stopping at the identified points to discuss the material. The teacher reminds the students of the importance of each person contributing something to the discussions. Here are examples from the first round of discussion:

Summarizer: The reading so far is about how manatees find their food.
Clarifier: It might be difficult for them to locate their food because of their small eyes.
Questioner: Do you think their small eyes affect their vision?
Predictor: I think the manatees' small eyes do affect their vision and might be one of the reasons they are becoming extinct.

D–Delivery

Reciprocal teaching highlights four comprehension processes: predicting, questioning, clarifying, and summarizing. It is advisable to teach the processes one at a time.

1. Choose a short passage from a text to use for demonstration and modeling.
2. Demonstrate one process at a time through several short readings from the passage. As students become familiar with the process, have them work in groups to read a selection of text and work on that one process. Follow this routine for each of the processes until all four have been introduced.
3. Once students have been exposed to all four processes, select a short passage to read while you model all four processes: *predict* what you believe will occur next; *generate questions* about the text that you or someone else might ask; stop and *attempt to clarify* words or sections in the text, talking through your confusion; and *summarize* what you believe are the most important ideas the author would want you to take away.
4. Once students understand how all four processes work together to help them make meaning from text, use the strategy as a class activity or in small groups with the students taking on more and more of the responsibility for implementing the strategy.

Reference

Palinscar, A. S., and A. Brown. 1986. Interactive teaching to promote independent learning from text. *The Reading Teacher* 39 (8): 771–77.

SKIMMING AND SCANNING

When to Teach		Group Size		Grade Level	
Before Reading	📖	One-on-One	👥	PreK–2	
During Reading	📖	Small Group	👥	3–5	🏫
After Reading	📖	Whole Group	👥	6–8	🏫

R–Rationale

Skimming and scanning helps students peruse material to be read so that they can activate and/or establish topic knowledge, formulate a hypothesis of the content (Pressley 2002), and quickly locate information. This strategy helps students see the value in "visiting" the text before, during, and after reading.

E–Explanation

Skimming requires students to quickly read through a text to determine what it will be about; it is a way for students to preview the material. Students learn how to rapidly move through a text by reading the title, the introduction, the first one or two sentences of each paragraph, followed by the conclusion or summary. Skimming can help students determine the main ideas in a text and then decide whether the information is useful for their purposes.

Scanning is a strategy that teaches students how to look for specific facts or details. There is no attempt to construct meaning from the text at this point. Instead, students are trying to locate information, such as key words, dates, names, or answers to specific questions. After the information is located, students can go back and read that segment of text more closely.

A–Application

The teacher models for students the process of skimming by walking them through the basic steps. She then reads aloud to students the introduction of a section on the classification of living things. She pauses and thinks aloud about the conclusions she has drawn thus far about what the section might be about. The teacher then reads the information found on a diagram in that section and the first one to two sentences of each paragraph of the section. Next, she pauses and asks students to turn and talk to each other about the information they have gained from what was read. Then the teacher continues perusing the next couple of sections and guides the students in drawing conclusions about why scientists group living things.

The teacher then uses the same section of text to reinforce the idea of scanning as a way to quickly read through a text to locate specific information. She guides students in scanning the text for answers to each of these questions, presented one at a time:

- What is a kingdom?
- How are monerans and protists the same?
- Why do scientists organize living things?

After students scan the section of text for each question, the teacher pauses and talks about what helped them to locate each piece of information quickly.

D–Delivery

Skimming and scanning can vary depending on the text, the students, and the purpose for reading. General steps for teaching students how to skim a text include these:

1. Introduce the text by telling students its title or heading.
2. Read the introduction of the section.
3. Read the first one to two sentences of each paragraph.
4. Read the conclusion or summary of this section of text.
5. Discuss what the main idea of the text seems to be.
6. During discussion, ask students to refer back to the text to justify their assessment of the main idea.

General steps for teaching students how to scan a text include these:

1. Tell students to scan a segment of text to locate specific information quickly (e.g., how to measure atmospheric conditions).
2. Explain that they should look through the text rapidly, noticing headings, boldfaced words, italicized words, or words that are in a different font size or style from that of the other words.
3. Tell students also to pay attention to margin notes or any pictures, diagrams, or other illustrations by reading the captions.
4. Once students have finished scanning the text, discuss what they learned.
5. Have students refer to the text to justify the answers they found.

Reference

Pressley, M. 2002. Metacognition and self-regulated comprehension. In *What research has to say about reading instruction* (3rd ed.), ed. A. E. Farstrup and S. J. Samuels, 291–309. Newark, DE: International Reading Association.

STORY BAGS

When to Teach		Group Size		Grade Level	
Before Reading		One-on-One	📖👤	PreK–2	🏫
During Reading	📖	Small Group	👥	3–5	🏫
After Reading	📖	Whole Group		6–8	🏫

R–Rationale

The story bag strategy requires students to think critically as they determine what artifacts will best represent a story. This strategy pushes students to analyze a text in order to come up with an appropriate artifact. It also provides an opportunity for writing as students explain the connection of the artifact to the story.

E–Explanation

The story bag strategy requires students to analyze a text they have read and then identify artifacts that represent the character(s), setting, theme, or events. This strategy is a form of story mapping, in which students identify graphic, pictorial, and/or symbolic representations of a story. Identifying the main ideas of the text and then integrating these ideas into a coherent whole (National Reading Panel 2000) helps students write a summary about the story bag. The added writing component involves students in explaining the connection of an artifact to the story.

   The story bag activity is best discussed prior to students starting a new book, because it prompts them to think about possible items they might want to include in the artifact bag once they have finished the story. Teachers can require students to include from five to ten artifacts, which can range from actual items to drawn pictures, to pictures the students take, to pictures they find on the Web, or to pictures they cut out of other resources. Students can create the artifacts using a combination of objects, and they can use objects from the world around them. For each item in the story bag, students could write a description on index cards that justifies how each relates to the element(s) of the story.

A–Application

After a two-week literature circle book study, the teacher instructs the reading groups to develop a story bag containing artifacts that represent key components of the text they read. The group that reads *The Watsons Go to Birmingham–1963* (Curtis 1995) included air freshener to represent the air freshener that was in the Watsons' car when they drove to Birmingham. They also included a small toy car to represent the Watsons' car, the Brown Bomber. A sheet of paper with the song title "Yakkety Yak" was used to represent the song the family played on the ultra-glide, a machine that plays records in the car, during their trip. In addition, the students completed a written summary explaining how each artifact is related to the book. The teacher displayed all the groups' books, story bags, and accompanying written summaries on a table in the reading area for other students to view.

Lindsey Schoolfield

D–Delivery

With story bags, students select artifacts to represent key elements of a story (e.g., characters, setting, problem, events, solution, theme). The artifacts can be literal as well as symbolic.

1. Prior to having students read a story, discuss with them that they will be asked to create a story bag after they finish reading the story. Tell them to think about what they could include in their story bag as they are reading the story. As an example, select a common fairy tale, and talk with students about the types of artifacts they could include to represent that story. Students can work with their whole group to create the story bag, or they can work independently.
2. Provide students with a sheet of paper on which to record possible artifacts, along with a space where they can write a short note to remind themselves of why it would be a good artifact to include.
3. After they have finished reading, ask students to select at least five artifacts to represent the story. They should include a written justification for each artifact, identifying the artifact and explaining in detail how the artifact is connected to the book. The written justification can be written on a note card and attached to the artifact, or students can include all the justifications on a one-page written narrative.
4. Ask students to decorate the front of the story bag with the title of the book, the author's name, and an illustration that represents the story.
5. Have students present their story bags to the rest of the class. They should show each artifact and clearly explain how the artifact is connected to the story.

References

Curtis, C. P. 1995. *The Watsons go to Birmingham–1963*. New York: Scholastic.
National Reading Panel. 2000. *Teaching children to read: An evidence-based assessment of the scientific research literature on reading and its implications for reading instruction* (NIH Publication No. 00-4769). Washington, DC: National Institute of Child Health and Human Development, National Institutes of Health.

STORY MAPS

When to Teach		Group Size		Grade Level	
Before Reading		One-on-One		PreK–2	
During Reading		Small Group		3–5	
After Reading		Whole Group		6–8	

R–Rationale

Story maps (Beck and McKeown 1981) help students in their understanding and use of story elements. This strategy helps students recognize that stories have a somewhat predictable "grammar," which readers can sense and use while reading to improve their comprehension. This sense of story also aids students when they write stories.

E–Explanation

Story mapping is a strategy that helps students use their understanding of narrative structure to analyze stories. Students are provided with a visual framework for analyzing a story based on story structure. There are numerous ways that a story can be graphically illustrated, but they should all be based on elements of story structure. Questions related to story structure often accompany the graphic to lead to more integrated comprehension. For example, instead of just having the words *setting, character,* and so on listed on the graphic, the teacher might include questions like "Where and when does the story take place?" "Who is the main character, and what does this character do?" Some story maps do not use a graphic but only a sequential line of questioning to lead students to a better understanding of the story. For example,

1. Where and when did the story take place?
2. Who was the main character?
3. What was the character's problem?
4. What did the character need to do?

This line of questioning would continue until the resolution and theme of the story were identified. Both types of story maps aid students in comprehension and in developing a sense of story, but most teachers use either the graphic story map or a combination of the graphic and the questions.

A–Application

After students read the story *Corduroy* (Freeman 1976), the teacher guides them in completing a story map. He distributes a story map to each student and displays one on the overhead for his use. He has the students put the title of the story and the name of the author in the center of their story maps. The teacher then asks the students a series of questions about the story:

1. The story took place at two main places. What were they?
2. Who were the two main characters?
3. What was the problem with Lisa buying Corduroy?
4. What did Corduroy try to do to fix the problem?
5. How did Corduroy get back to his shelf?
6. What happened the next morning?
7. After Lisa took Corduroy home, what did she do to fix his problem?

After each question, the students respond, class discussion follows if needed, and then both students and teacher write the information in the appropriate section of their story maps. Once the story map is complete, the teacher puts the students in small groups to discuss the story, using the story map to guide their conversation. The students then collaboratively produce a written retelling of the story.

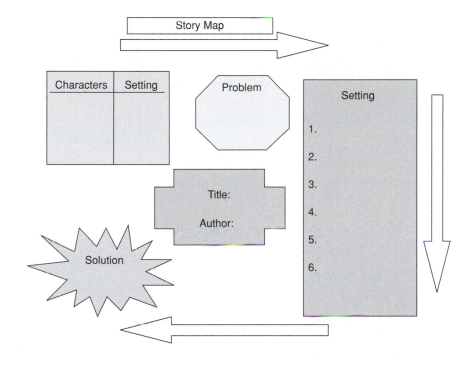

D–Delivery

Story maps can be created for short stories and for longer pieces of narrative texts.

1. Read a story to the students, or have them read a story independently or in small groups. When initially using story maps, be sure that the selected story has a clear illustration of story structure and preferably only one setting, problem, and so on. After students have a thorough understanding of story and are familiar with the story map strategy, stories can have multiple settings, problems, and so on and can be more complex in style.
2. Discuss the story in general, paying attention to the common elements of narrative text.
3. Distribute blank story maps to the students. Simple graphics are better to begin with, but students later will enjoy working with story maps in a variety of shapes and designs.
4. Have students fill in key information from the story. Model the process initially while the students complete their story maps.
5. Consider having the students use the story map to write a retelling of the story.

References

Beck, I., and M. McKeown. 1981. Developing questions that promote comprehension: The story map. *Language Arts* 58: 913–18.

Freeman, D. 1976. *Corduroy*. New York: Puffin Books.

STORY PYRAMIDS

When to Teach		Group Size		Grade Level	
Before Reading		One-on-One	👥	PreK–2	🏫
During Reading		Small Group	👥	3–5	🏫
After Reading	📖	Whole Group	👥	6–8	🏫

R–Rationale

Story pyramids foster understanding of story elements and help students in summarizing narrative text. This strategy helps develop analytical skills as students dig deeper into text in order to structure their understanding of what was read according to a required pattern. This strategy also builds oral language and vocabulary because students have to choose their words wisely. Instruction in story structure "from which the reader learns to ask who, what, where, when, and why questions" (National Reading Panel 2000, 4–6) has been shown to be effective in impacting a reader's comprehension.

E–Explanation

Story pyramids are an after-reading strategy that promotes critical analysis of a story and the precise use of language to describe certain parts of story grammar. The story pyramid is an excellent reading extension activity because students must draw on their knowledge of both story structure and story language. Students write a summary of the story, using a set number of words for various elements of the story. Their writing is organized in the shape of a triangle or pyramid, with each line having a required pattern. The pattern may change from one pyramid to another but generally consists of the following:

1. Name of the main character
2. Two words describing the main character
3. Three words describing the setting
4. Four words stating the problem
5. Five words describing the first event
6. Six words describing the second event
7. Seven words describing the third event
8. Eight words stating the solution

A–Application

After reading the story *Rosie's Walk* (Hutchins 1971), the teacher puts students into groups. They discuss the story among themselves, making sure that they are clear on the main characters, setting, problem, events, and resolution. The teacher instructs the groups to choose just one of the main characters from the story—Rosie or the fox. The teacher then passes out paper with lines that form the shape of a pyramid. The students collaboratively complete the story pyramid, drawing on their knowledge of the story and their ability to choose their words carefully to fit the pattern. All the groups then share their story pyramids, noting how each one might be different yet still provide the same basic information about the story. The following is a sample from a second grader:

Rosie's Walk
Rosie
doesn't know
walking the farm
fox hungry for Rosie
fox tries to get Rosie
fox follows but always gets hurt
bees chase the fox away from Rosie
Rosie gets home safely in time for dinner

D–Delivery

Story pyramids require students to put their understanding of a story into succinct language following a given pattern, which may vary.

1. Read a story aloud to the class or have students read a common selection themselves.
2. Engage the class in a brief discussion about the story, having them pay attention to the story elements.
3. Distribute a blank story pyramid to the students. Have them complete the pyramid as an independent activity, have them work together in pairs or small groups, or have them work as a whole class while you complete the pyramid on a large chart or on the overhead.

name of the main character
two words describing the main character
three words describing the setting
four words stating the problem
five words describing the first event
six words describing the second event
seven words describing the third event
eight words stating the solution

References

Hutchins, P. 1971. *Rosie's walk.* New York: Aladdin.

National Reading Panel. 2000. *Teaching children to read: An evidence-based assessment of the scientific research literature on reading and its implications for reading instruction* (NIH Publication No. 00-4769). Washington, DC: National Institute of Child Health and Human Development, National Institutes of Health.

Section VII

Writing

Writing is an effective means of communication and an essential part of literacy instruction. Writing requires making connections, constructing meaning, exploring thinking, and creating new knowledge (Bromley 2007). This activity can range from something as simple as responding to literature, such as students do in journals and literature logs, to something that is much more complex and requires more in-depth acts of composing.

The classroom writing environment is critical for effective writing instruction. Students need to be immersed in an environment rich with words—both oral and in print. Students also need to feel comfortable sharing their writing with others—the thinking and brainstorming involved in the writing as well as the finished product. A writing community encourages student writing.

Writers also need direct, intentional instruction in writing and adequate time to write (Tompkins 2004). Students need to learn how to use the traits of writing (Culhum 2003) to write in a variety of forms and for different purposes. Good teachers balance response or free writing and the writing process.

It is important that students understand what is involved in the process of writing, which has undergone many changes in the past twenty years. Certain acts of composing are present in almost all variations of the process: planning, drafting, aligning, revising, and monitoring. Tierney and Pearson (1983) discuss how both reading and writing are reflected within these acts of composing:

- Planning—A writer plans what will be written, and a reader plans what will be read. As a reader reads and a writer writes, goals may emerge, be changed, or be discovered.
- Drafting—As readers and writers deal with the print on the page, they are refining meaning. A writer makes decisions about what information to include or not include, while a reader fills in gaps or makes connections. In this phase, instead of looking at reading or writing as a piecemeal experience, readers and writers should strive for the fit between the whole and the parts and among the parts.
- Aligning—Alignment refers to how the reader or writer relates to the author or audience. Alignment has two facets: the stance readers or writers assume when working together with an author or audience and the roles in which readers or writers immerse themselves as they move forward with the topic.
- Revising—Revisions are integral to reading and writing. If readers are to develop some control over and sense of discovery with the models of meaning they build, they must approach text with the same deliberation, time, and reflection that writers employ as they revise a text.
- Monitoring—This stage of the composing process involves an awareness of whether the planning, drafting, aligning, and revising were done correctly. Our monitor tells us when we have done well or not done well or when we need to start over. It requires readers and writers to distance themselves from the text in order to evaluate the work that was done.

Graves (1983, 1994) emphasizes the importance of student engagement in relevant writing opportunities that involve the recursive steps of the writing process. It is also important to remember that the components of the writing process are initially explained in sequence but that writing is not always a linear process.

Effective writing teachers use metacognitive strategies to guide their students in honing their craft and enriching their abilities as authors (Calkins, 1994; Israel et al. 2005). Effective teaching of the writing craft helps students develop an awareness of what writers do when they write. There are numerous skills involved in being a good writer, as well as a variety of instructional strategies for developing these skills. However, there are three key practices teachers should remember when planning writing instruction (Israel and Block 2005, 132).

- Leading students in rich discussions about writing using quality literature.
- Fostering individual student enthusiasm for writing.
- Teaching students practical strategies that specifically and personally enhance their writing craft.

The goal of a writing program should be to develop students who enjoy writing and who can write in a range of forms and for a variety of purposes and audiences (Bromley 2007).

References

Bromley, K. 2007. Best practices in teaching writing. In *Best practices in literacy instruction* (3rd ed.), ed. L. B. Gambrell, L. L. Morrow, and M. Pressley, 243–63. New York: Guilford.

Calkins, L. M. 1994. *The art of teaching writing*. Portsmouth, NH: Heinemann.

Culhum, R. 2003. *6+1 traits of writing: The complete guide: Grades 3 and up*. New York: Scholastic.

Graves, D. 1983. *Writing: Teachers and children at work*. Portsmouth, NH: Heinemann.

Graves, D. 1994. *A fresh look at writing*. Portsmouth, NH: Heinemann.

Israel, S. E., and C. C. Block. 2005. *Reading First and beyond: The complete guide for teachers and literacy coaches*. Thousand Oaks, CA: Corwin Press.

Israel, S. E., C. C. Block, K. Bauserman, and K. Kinucan-Welsch. 2005. *Metacognition in literacy learning: Theory, assessment, instruction, and professional development*. Mahwah, NJ: Erlbaum.

Tierney, R. J., and P. D. Pearson. 1983. Toward a composing model of reading. Language Arts 60: 568–80.

Tompkins, G. E. 2004. *Teaching writing: Balancing process and product*. Upper Saddle River, NJ: Prentice Hall.

ALPHABET BOOKS

When to Teach		Group Size		Grade Level	
Before Reading		One-on-One		PreK–2	
During Reading		Small Group		3–5	
After Reading		Whole Group		6–8	

R–Rationale

The alphabet book strategy involves students in creating an alphabet book about a given topic. It works best with a more global topic, since students are expected to find a topically related word for each letter of the alphabet. This strategy lends itself to robust vocabulary instruction (Beck, McKeown, and Kucan 2002), since students have the opportunity for meaningful exploration of words. In addition, when students create alphabet books, they also move through stages of the writing process (Dahl and Farnan 1998; Peterson 2003) as they research and gather information, draft their books, revise and edit, and then complete the final publication.

E–Explanation

The alphabet book can be created in a variety of ways:

- On poster paper
- In a big book format
- As an eight-page book

Students are given a topic related to an overall unit and then work with a partner or small group to make an alphabet book. Students are asked to find words for each letter of the alphabet, or they can choose eight to ten letters of the alphabet that they want to represent. On each actual page of the alphabet book, students should identify the particular letter of the alphabet and then clearly identify the word(s) related to the topic. Students can also include illustrations that relate to the word(s) listed on the page, as well as a sentence for each word on the page.

A–Application

An excerpt from an aphabet book is shown here for the letters *Bb* and *Dd*. In this case, the student represented each letter with four different vocabulary words and provided a picture to illustrate each one. The alphabet vocabulary book could be used to help students extend their understanding of the key words by having them select a word or words and writing three to four sentences that provide more information and detail related to the word(s).

World War II

| **Bb** | bomb  | Bataan |
| | Blitzkrieg | Benito Mussolini |

| **Dd** | D-DAY | dictator |
| | Douglas MacArthur | Dwight D. Eisenhower |

D–Delivery

It helps to show students examples of different alphabet books to help them get ideas about how they could organize their own alphabet books. If the alphabet book will be done as a group project, the teacher and students might decide together on one particular format so that the design elements are consistent across all groups. These are general guidelines for creating alphabet books:

1. Decide whether students will work independently, with a partner, or in a small group to complete the project.
2. Assign the topic that students will use to develop their alphabet books.
3. Assign students particular letters of the alphabet.
4. Discuss with students what elements should be included for each letter of the alphabet:
    a. Letter of the alphabet
    b. Certain number of words per letter
    c. Illustrations for each word
    d. Perhaps three to four sentences that elaborate on each word
5. Have students work together to research information they need to complete their part of the alphabet book. A graphic organizer is helpful to keep track of this information:

Letter	Word	Possible Pictures/ Graphics

6. Have students create a draft of their part of the alphabet book and get feedback from peers as well as the teacher.
7. Have students write the final draft, and then combine all of the pages to make a class alphabet book.

References

Beck, K. L., M. G. McKeown, and L. Kucan. 2002. *Bringing words to life: Robust vocabulary instruction*. New York: Guilford.

Dahl, K. L., and N. Farnan. 1998. *Children's writing: Perspectives from research*. Newark, DE: International Reading Association.

Peterson, S. 2003. *Untangling some knots in K–8 writing instruction*. Newark, DE: International Reading Association.

INTERACTIVE WRITING

When to Teach		Group Size		Grade Level	
Before Reading		One-on-One		PreK–2	
During Reading		Small Group		3–5	
After Reading		Whole Group		6–8	

R–Rationale

Interactive writing, developed by educators at Ohio State University (Pinnell and McCarrier 1994), is a form of the more familiar term *shared writing*. It is a powerful strategy for teaching many skills simultaneously: determining text, matching speech to print, hearing sounds in words (i.e., phonemic awareness), understanding conventions of print, using phonics, and so on. Interactive writing also helps pull reluctant writers into the writing process.

E–Explanation

Interactive writing involves a sharing of the pen between teacher and students. Students are actively engaged in the planning and construction of text and, to the greatest degree possible, the writing of text. The teacher guides the process and the pacing of the writing, providing assistance and instruction when needed. Interactive writing can be completed in a variety of formats but generally works better in a small group so that all students can participate in the process. The text created is usually a sentence or short composition about a story read or any shared experience. The teacher and students orally compose the piece to be written and then share in recording it on chart paper. Students contribute as much as they can to the writing (e.g., a letter, part of a word, a whole word), with the teacher providing only the elements of spelling they have not yet been taught.

A–Application

After reading a text about making kites, the teacher and students hold a prewriting discussion in order to decide what they would like to write about the text. After much negotiating, a sentence is decided: "Kites fly high in the sky." Initially, only one sentence is negotiated, but this activity can extend into longer compositions as students develop their skills. The negotiated sentence is written piece-by-piece on chart paper with magic markers. Both teacher and students share the recording task. Students write as much as they can, with the teacher supplying word parts that the students have not yet learned. During the sharing of the pen, the sentence is repeated over and over so that students can hear the sounds as they contribute to the writing. If errors are made, they are covered up with removable correction tape, but the teacher might engage the students in a practice lesson before correcting the error. Dialogue during the entire process is very important, as the following example demonstrates:

Teacher: The first word is *kites*. Say the word *kites* slowly.
That begins with the same letter as your name, Katie.
You be the first writer.
Class, where do you think Katie should begin?
That's right. She should begin here at the edge of the paper.
This is the first letter in our sentence, so what kind of letter should Katie write? Yes, she should use a capital letter.
Good job, Katie.
Now say the word *kite* again.
What do you think the next letter will be? Yes, it is an *i*.
Who can write the letter *i* next to the capital *K*?

It is extremely important that students are engaged in the writing experience. As the teacher becomes more familiar with what individual students know and can do, the more they can contribute at one time. However, every student can contribute in some way, even if it is initially only to serve as the placeholder between words.

D–Delivery

Students and the teacher share the pen as they write messages created by the students.

1. Prepare and gather materials: colored markers—different colors for each student, with the teacher reserving the black; white correction tape for errors; chart paper—folded in two sections (top and bottom); magnetic letters or letter tiles; and a pointer.
2. Have students assemble around the chart and distribute the colored markers. Have students write their names with their colored markers on the bottom of the chart. This allows you to match the writing to the student.
3. Provide a stimulus for the writing, perhaps derived from a read-aloud book, field trip, class activity, and so on.
4. Have students orally create a sentence or short "story" (two to three sentences) in response to the stimulus.
5. Have students repeat the passage several times, segmenting it into words. Then help them write the passage word by word or letter by letter, depending on the level of the students. Allow the students to provide as much of the writing as they can; fill in only where they need assistance. After each word is written, have a student serve as the spacer to mark the space between words. Have students reread the passage from the beginning each time a new word is completed.
   - Use magnetic letters when students need assistance forming a word.
   - Use the bottom half of the folded chart for students to practice forming their letters, if needed.
   - Use the pointer to point to each word as the students reread the passage.
6. After the writing is completed, make it available to the students: displayed on the wall, placed in a center, and so forth.

Reference

Pinnell, G. S., and A. McCarrier. 1994. Interactive writing: A transition tool for assisting children in learning to read and write. In *Getting reading right from the start: Effective early literacy interventions*, ed. E. Hiebert and B. Taylor, 149–70. Needham, MA: Allyn & Bacon.

JOURNALS

When to Teach		Group Size		Grade Level	
Before Reading	📖	One-on-One	👥	PreK–2	🏫
During Reading		Small Group	👥	3–5	🏫
After Reading	📖	Whole Group	👥	6–8	🏫

R–Rationale

Journals are a way for students to record reactions to literature. Other names for this type of strategy include *reading journal*, *reading log*, *literature log*, *literature response journal*, and *reading response log*. Journals give students a nonthreatening place where they can use writing to explore what they are learning and what they are feeling (Richardson and Morgan 2003; Routman 1991).

E–Explanation

A journal is designed to move students beyond basic summary and recall of information. Students can use this format to do many other things (adapted from Routman 1991):

- Respond to an open-ended question.
- Reflect on personal reactions while reading.
- Choose several unknown vocabulary words and investigate their meanings.
- Illustrate a part of the text.
- Examine the author's style and motives.
- Freewrite to describe what is best about the book.
- Imagine another point of view.
- Make up a question(s) for discussion.
- Respond to a final question after reading the entire book.

A–Application

A teacher helps her students learn how to respond in their literature response journals by talking about a book they are reading. She uses the chalkboard, overhead, or projection system to display a written response about the book, and she talks aloud as she writes the response to help students understand how they, too, can write and reflect about what they are reading.

Another teacher, Linda Rief (1992), emphasizes in her book *Seeking Diversity: Language Arts with Adolescents* that readers also want a response to what they write. Rief addresses the issue of how a teacher can respond to a large number of journals by sharing her own experience. She collected her students' journals every two weeks for the first couple of months and responded to them herself. But after three or four months, she established a rotating schedule by which students got a response from a peer of their choice the first week, from her the second week, from a parent or sibling the third week, and then again from her the fourth week. Another option is to assign students designated days when they turn in their journals for review. For example, if there are twenty-four students in a class, six students could be assigned Monday, another six Tuesday, and so forth. This would leave Friday open so that other types of grading could be done over the weekend. The teacher could also plan a personal conference with students on their designated pick-up day.

D–Delivery

Students can use a variety of mediums to respond in writing to what they are reading in their literature circles. Four possibilities include traditional paper and pencil, email, discussion boards, and weblogs.

1. Have students record their thoughts and ideas about a text using traditional paper-and-pencil formats, such as notebooks or folders with loose-leaf paper. Folders with brads work well because students can easily add paper as needed throughout the year.
2. Have students use email to facilitate conversation with you or with other students in the group. Consider having students compose their responses in a word-processed document and then copy and paste it to email.
3. Set up discussion boards so that students can post and respond to others in their group. Have students access a forum, which could be their book, and then post a response. Discussion boards allow students to easily read through and respond to what others have said. For example, the BlackBoard platform (http://www.blackboard.com) has an option to create discussion boards that are easily managed by an instructor. Students log in with a username and password from home or school, and then access the discussion board and post a response. Once students have finished with a literature circle, their postings can be archived. This type of platform presents a more controlled environment for students to work in.
4. Create weblogs, or blogs, that can include text, pictures, audio, Flash, and PowerPoint slideshows or Excel spreadsheets for linking. Blogs can be created with a minimum of technology know-how and can utilize free resources:
    *   Blogger—http://www.blogger.com
    *   moTime—http://www.motime.com
    *   tBlog—http://www.tblog.com
5. Regardless of the format, provide journal starters to help students when they first begin responding. Because they often have no idea what to write, suggestions help them begin the process. Students who have not had opportunities to write about a book they are reading often say, "It was very good. I liked it a lot." However, with explanation and modeling and daily opportunities to respond, the quality of their writing will grow exponentially.
6. Evaluate the journals for depth of response, CUPS (capitalization, usage, punctuation, and spelling), and participation.

References

Richardson, J. S., and R. F. Morgan. 2003. *Reading to learn in the content areas* (5th ed.). Belmont, CA: Wadsworth/ Thomson Learning.

Rief, L. 1992. *Seeking diversity: Language arts with adolescents.* Portsmouth, NH: Heinemann.

Routman, R. 1991. *Invitations: Changing as teachers and learners K–12.* Portsmouth, NH: Heinemann.

LEARNING LOGS

When to Teach		Group Size		Grade Level	
Before Reading	📖	One-on-One	👥	PreK–2	🏫
During Reading	📖	Small Group	👥	3–5	🏫
After Reading	📖	Whole Group	👥	6–8	🏫

R–Rationale

Learning logs are tools designed to help students think about concepts in reading, reflect on learning that has occurred, and process new understandings. This strategy is an ongoing record of what is being learned (Olness 2007). Learning logs are a simple and effective way to get students to write in content-area classrooms. They ask students to keep a record of ideas or questions they have about a topic or processes they used when reading a text.

E–Explanation

Students reflect on what they have read or discussed by writing short responses to a question or prompt. Learning logs serve as academic reflections of students' learning and help students understand the relevance of taking time to process information.

A–Application

The teacher has his students respond in their learning logs for about five to ten minutes at least once a week. He encourages the students to write questions they may have about a topic and to share what they have learned. The teacher then reviews what they have written to get a better idea about what they are thinking. It helps him spot any misunderstandings.

The teacher sometimes uses learning logs as a prereading activity to activate prior knowledge about a topic. For example, if the class is beginning a unit on the English colonies, he might ask, "Why were the English colonies founded?" This gives students time to write about what they already know about this topic. If the topic is one they have not encountered before, students write whatever questions they have about it.

As a during-reading activity, the teacher asks students to make a prediction or draw a conclusion about what was read or to write down what they are confused about. Any "confusions" are revisited at the end of the lesson to be sure they have been resolved. The teacher also uses learning logs as an after-reading activity to focus attention on what was read for the day's lesson. He uses a prompt such as, "Write about something new that you learned today."

D–Delivery

Learning logs provide a way for students to respond to what they are reading in texts.

1. Have students create their logs by stapling pages together or using a folder with brads and pockets and then personalize them. Learning log responses can also be one-time reflections, which are not compiled in a cumulative location.
2. Have students make entries in their learning logs periodically while covering new information. Stop at key points in the lesson for students to respond, or allow them to respond at will. Use a variety of prompts to generate thoughts, or pose open-ended questions.
3. Read and respond to the entries 1–2 times a week to answer students' questions and/or clarify any confusion.

Reference

Olness, R. 2007. *Using literature to enhance content area instruction*. Newark, DE: International Reading Association.

RAFT

When to Teach		Group Size		Grade Level	
Before Reading	📖	One-on-One	👥	PreK–2	🏫
During Reading		Small Group	👥	3–5	🏫
After Reading	📖	Whole Group	👥	6–8	🏫

R–Rationale

Writing can be an effective way to help students think about the topic being studied or the material being read. The RAFT strategy (Santa 1988) is designed to encourage students to share their understanding of the content in a creative, imaginative, and critical way.

E–Explanation

RAFT is an acronym: **R**—*role* of the writer; **A**—*audience* for the writer; **F**—*format* of the writing; **T**—*topic* to be addressed in the writing. This strategy allows students to respond from a viewpoint other than their own, to an audience other than themselves or the teacher, and in a form other than the basic answer to a question. RAFT writing can be done in any subject area and in a variety of combinations. For example, the role, audience, and format can be the same for all members of the class, or different students or groups of students can portray different roles, write to different audiences, and use different formats to portray their understanding of the content.

A–Application

After students read the book *Corduroy* by Don Freeman, one language arts teacher had some students assume the role of Corduroy, who needed to tell someone about his adventures looking for the lost button. Their format was a letter to a "stuffed" friend who once lived in the department store. Other members of the class assumed the role of Lisa and told in a diary format how she felt about leaving Corduroy in the department store. Another teacher with a math class studying geometric shapes had the students take the role of different shapes and write letters convincing the teacher of the important functions those shapes played in the world.

Examples of Possible RAFT Assignments

Role	Audience	Format	Topic
Citizen	Legislator	Letter	Vote for recycling
Comma	7th grade students	Job description	Use in sentences
Scientist	Charles Darwin	Letter	Refute theory of evolution
Cracker	Other crackers	Travel guide	Journey through digestive system
Lungs	Cigarettes	Complaint	Effects of smoking

D–Delivery

RAFT is generally considered an after-reading strategy but can also be used before reading to determine students' background knowledge.

1. Help students analyze important ideas or information learned from reading a story, textbook passage, or other resource.
2. Present RAFT to the students, and explain the four components: *role* of the writer, *audience* to whom the writing is directed, *format* of the writing, and *topic* on which the writing will focus.
3. Have students generate examples and discuss the four elements until everyone understands what must be taken into consideration with each one.
4. Have students use RAFT as they plan their writing. Have all students do the same assignment the first time. Later, allow different students to take on different roles, writing formats, and so on.

References

Santa, C. M. 1988. *Content reading including secondary systems*. Dubuque, IA: Kendall Hunt.
Freeman, D. 1976. *Corduroy*. New York: Puffin Books.

REAP

When to Teach		Group Size		Grade Level	
Before Reading	📖	One-on-One	👥	PreK–2	
During Reading	📖	Small Group	👤	3–5	🏫
After Reading	📖	Whole Group	👥	6–8	🏫

R–Rationale

REAP (Eanet and Manzo 1976) is a strategy designed to help students internalize content as they work their way through text. REAP increases comprehension while strengthening students' ability to think at higher levels of understanding when engaged in text.

E–Explanation

REAP is an acronym for four stages of reading: read, encode, annotate, and ponder. This strategy helps students read and understand a text by having them think about ways to represent the main ideas of the reading selection in both the author's and their own words.

A–Application

A teacher has her students use the REAP process to help them analyze, question, and review their understanding of the San Francisco earthquake. The students first read the text. Next, they record the gist of what was read using their own understanding at this point rather than specific facts from the text. They then annotate the text by writing down the main idea and the author's message using the text for specific facts as needed. Last, they ponder what they read, making connections and considering questions they might have had about the topic.

REAP	
Read Title: *The San Francisco Earthquake*	**E**ncode The earthquake that hit San Francisco was one of America's most devastating natural disasters and helped us see the need for better ways to prepare and protect ourselves from future earthquakes.
Annotate The earthquake was one of the strongest to ever hit North America. Many people were killed, and the destruction was massive. Scientists still cannot prevent earthquakes, but we are now better prepared to handle them.	**P**onder The devastation created by the San Francisco earthquake reminds me of when Hurricane Katrina hit New Orleans. I wonder if Louisiana is now better prepared to handle hurricanes.

D–Delivery

Teacher modeling of this strategy, followed by guided student practice, will support students' understanding of the strategy as well as increase their content knowledge of the material being read. The steps provided here indicate that students complete the strategy independently, but it is important to remember that it has first been modeled for them as well as practiced in small groups or with partners until all students are ready to apply it individually.

1. Have students read the text on their own.
2. Have students encode the text by putting the gist of what they read into their own words.
3. Have students annotate the text by writing down the main ideas and the author's message.
4. Have students ponder what they have read in order to make connections and/or develop questions about the topic. All parts of the strategy might be enhanced by having students work together, but this area especially benefits when students talk to others about what they have read.

Reference

Eanet, M., and A. Manzo. 1976. R.E.A.P.—A strategy for improving reading/writing study skills. *Journal of Reading* 19: 647–52.

SPAWN

When to Teach		Group Size		Grade Level	
Before Reading		One-on-One	👥	PreK–2	
During Reading		Small Group	👥	3–5	🏫
After Reading	📖	Whole Group	👥	6–8	🏫

R–Rationale

SPAWN (Martin, Martin, and O'Brien 1984) encourages students to individually or collaboratively examine complex issues and extend their thinking related to content reading. This strategy provides writing prompts in five categories; the thinking and writing involved can be used as a springboard for class discussions and problem solving.

E–Explanation

SPAWN is an acronym: **S**—special powers (i.e., students are given the power to change a certain aspect of the topic or text); **P**—problem solving (i.e., students write solutions to problems posed by the text or teacher); **A**—alternative viewpoints (i.e., students write about the topic from a specific perspective); **W**—what if (i.e., the teacher makes a change to the topic, and students write based on the change); and **N**—next (i.e., students write in anticipation of what will be discussed later). The strategy allows a teacher to create numerous thought-provoking prompts related to the topic being studied and encourages students to write responses that move beyond simple answering of questions to higher-order thinking.

A–Application

After students read a selection in the basal reading text, the teacher asks them to respond to a special powers(s) prompt: "You have the power to change the setting of the story from New York City to rural Mississippi. How would this change the ending of the story?" The next (N) prompt also encourages students to anticipate and problem solve; the teacher asks them to consider a certain point in the story and to write what might have happened next if the character had responded differently.

   Another teacher uses the SPAWN prompts to expand his students' understanding of Christopher Columbus and the discovery of the New World.

S—You have the power to change an important event leading up to the discovery of the New World. Describe what you are changing and what the consequences of the change are.
P—How do you think the Indians felt when Columbus took some of their family members with them?
A—Imagine that you are the chief of the Indian tribe living where Columbus landed. Write a description of the "discovery" from the chief's point of view.

W—What might have happened if the Indians had not welcomed Columbus?

N—We learned yesterday that Columbus left the New World carrying several members of the Indian tribe with him. What do you think happened when they arrived in Spain?

D–Delivery

SPAWN encourages students to extend their thinking related to content material.

1. Explain the SPAWN acronym and process to students, making sure they understand each prompt.
2. Determine the kind of thinking desired, and select the category of SPAWN that best matches that kind of thinking. For example, if you want students to look at the content in a different way, use the alternative viewpoints (A) prompt. Also consider dividing the class into five groups and letting each respond to a different prompt.
3. Have students read, work with, and research the topic.
4. Have students work individually or collaboratively on the writing assignment. In most cases they should complete the writing in ten to fifteen minutes. Remember that this is informal writing and should not be graded as formal writing.

Reference

Martin, C., M. Martin, and D. O'Brien. 1984. Spawning ideas for writing in the content areas. *Reading World* 11: 11–15.

WRITING FRAMES

When to Teach		Group Size		Grade Level	
Before Reading		One-on-One	👥	PreK–2	🏫
During Reading		Small Group	👥	3–5	🏫
After Reading	📖	Whole Group	👥	6–8	🏫

R–Rationale

Writing frames provide a safety net for young and/or reluctant writers. They help give students a framework for their writing, freeing them from worrying about conventions, format, and so on, so that they can concentrate on ideas. The general objectives are to help students realize that they can write, help them see ways to organize their thoughts while writing, and provide techniques needed to develop ideas (Pottle 1988).

E–Explanation

Writing frames have evolved over time and taken on characteristics of other writing strategies (e.g., learning logs, story prompts). Initially, writing frames were partially completed paragraphs that offered students a framework and guide for their writing while encouraging them to incorporate their own words and ideas into the frame. These frames were also used to help students recognize that writing is a process. In addition, writing frames can be used as a brainstorming technique, a model for writing a rough draft of a finished product, or a simple writing activity just to get students into writing. The example and procedures described in Application and Delivery represent the simple basic writing frame that utilizes partial paragraphs designed to help students get their thoughts on paper while moving them to a better understanding of the writing process. Two examples of other forms of writing frames are provided after these two sections.

A–Application

To initiate the writing process, the third-grade teacher decides to use writing frames. She prepares a short frame to guide her students' thinking and passes it out to them along with the following directions: "Read the frame completely, and then fill in the blanks with appropriate words. Feel free to rearrange words as long as they still make sense. Read the finished text carefully to check your work, and give it a title. Then rewrite the text on your lined paper." She also reminds the students to leave margins, use appropriate spacing between words, and write neatly.

> We all need someone to _____ . Some people go to their _____ or to their
> _____ when they need help. I always talk to _____ because I know that _____.
> We have known each other for _____ . We met when _____. It didn't take me long to
> know that _____. I am glad that I have _____ to help me when _____.

D–Delivery

Writing frames vary in design, but all offer students an opportunity to become writers.

1. Select a topic and write a frame (e.g., watching television, going shopping with friends). Keep the initial frames short, requiring students to add only a couple of words (similar to the cloze strategy). Over time make the frames more open-ended so that students are encouraged to add more of their own ideas. Consider writing a frame around a story that students have read; provide part of the text, and let the students complete the rest in a type of written retelling.
2. Explain the process to the students. Let students know that everyone's finished product will be different.
3. Distribute the frame to students, and give these directions:
   a. Read the frame completely before beginning.
   b. Fill in the blanks with appropriate words. Feel free to rearrange words as long as they still make sense.
   c. Read the finished text carefully to check your work.
   d. Give your text a title.
   e. Rewrite the text on lined paper. Be sure to leave margins, use appropriate spacing between words, and write neatly.
4. Have students share their work with partners or the class.

Story Frame

Story title _____

The story takes place
_____
_____

It really begins when
_____
_____

The problem is
_____
_____

The first thing that happens is
_____
_____

Then
_____
_____

After that,
_____
_____

The problem is solved when
_____
_____

Story Frame

Complete these frames using complete sentences. Then put the information from all the frames together on lined paper. Ready your text carefully, adding words where needed to help make the writing flow.

Setting	Characters

The problem	The first main event

Next event	Solution

Reference

Pottle, J. L. 1988. *Writing frames: 40 activities for learning the writing process*. Portland, ME: J. Weston Walch.

Section VIII

VIPs

Literacy strategies should be taught explicitly to students in order to help them become more proficient readers. In a comprehensive literacy program, students are exposed to a myriad of strategies designed to strengthen their development in a variety of areas. Previous sections in this text have dealt with strategies that focused on a specific literacy skill—oral language, phonemic awareness, phonics, fluency, vocabulary, comprehension, and writing. Certain reading strategies, however, do not fit as nicely within a focus area but are more overarching in nature. These very important practices and strategies (VIPs) help make up a flexible framework that is useful in conceptualizing a reading curriculum. The elements of the framework, or the VIPs we've chosen to include, involve practices that encompass scaffolding points of reading to, with, and by students.

- Read-aloud (To) allows students to hear quality literature read to them. The teacher is in full control of the reading in this case.
- Shared reading (To and With) enables students, with the support of other students and the teacher, to read materials that may be too difficult for them to read independently. Here the teacher and students share control of the reading.
- Guided reading (By) gives students teacher guidance with minimal support as they read materials written on their instructional level. In this situation the child is mostly in control of the reading, with the teacher providing support when needed.
- Independent reading (By) allows students time to practice their reading using a book of their choosing. The student is in full control of the reading.
- Literature circles (By) allow students to get together and discuss a story or book they have read and to go into more detail by using each other's comments and questions to dig deeper into the text. Students are in control of the reading and discussion with teacher assistance only as needed or requested.

Effective teachers teach strategies when students need them, in the context of authentic reading or writing activities (Allington 2001; Fountas and Pinnell 2006). These VIP strategies, in conjunction with the other strategies in this book, will help teachers keep students actively engaged as they learn important literacy skills.

References

Allington, R. L. 2001. *What really matters for struggling readers: Designing research-based reading programs*. New York: Longman.

Fountas, I. C., and G. S. Pinnell. 2006. *The Fountas & Pinnell leveled book list, K–8*. Portsmouth, NH: Heinemann.

READ-ALOUD

When to Teach		Group Size		Grade Level	
Before Reading	📖	One-on-One	👤	PreK–2	🏫
During Reading	📖	Small Group	👥	3–5	🏫
After Reading	📖	Whole Group	👥	6–8	🏫

R–Rationale

Reading aloud to students improves their reading, writing, speaking, and listening—and best of all, their attitudes about reading (Trelease 1995). Reading aloud is one of the most influential factors in helping students become proficient readers. According to Trelease, it "provides a model for strong oral language, provides an understanding of how print works, builds vocabulary, develops a knowledge of letters and letter-sound relations, develops a sense of story, develops an understanding of story structure, and builds a positive attitude and love of books" (97).

E–Explanation

Read-aloud is used here as the concept of an adult reading a book to a student or group of students (Trelease 1995). This strategy is appropriate across grade levels, with middle and high school students as well as with young students. The read-aloud method should be part of the daily routine in all grades, since it is a wonderful way to share a variety of literature with students and open the world of reading to them. "Read aloud can stand alone and be used strictly for relaxation and enjoyment; but when utilized for a more direct instructional purpose, it can be utilized as a springboard for numerous literacy activities" (Cummins and Stewart 2006 p. 98). An interactive read-aloud facilitates this as it is a planned, instructional strategy that can focus on certain aspects of literacy development. Interactive read-alouds can promote "intimate familiarity with a story, enhance enjoyment of stories, allow for positive social interaction, and provide rehearsal of comprehension strategies" (Barrentine 1996, 53).

A–Application

To start an interactive read-aloud, the teacher gathers the students comfortably around him. He then builds background knowledge necessary for the students to understand the story. He also sets the scene by having the students look at the book cover and make predictions about the setting and the characters, and he points out the title and author of the story. Thus, he involves the students in exchanging information and sets a relaxed, comfortable atmosphere for the read-aloud session.

When the teacher reads the story, he provides information about it, notices particulars about the characters and other story elements, and helps students piece together the larger picture. Dialogue between teacher and students is an essential component of an interactive read-aloud. The teacher continues to encourage students' comments by pausing periodically to let them share their ideas about the book. This type of interaction can help students notice things about the book that they might not have noticed otherwise. The teacher also asks students to share their predictions about what might happen next in the story; this allows him to take advantage of teachable moments to reinforce skills and strategies. The teacher is constantly aware of when to build students' background knowledge so that they can make connections with the text. By the end of the story, the teacher has assisted students in pulling together more than just overall comprehension of the story as collective sharing facilitates the construct of more complex understanding.

D–Delivery

Because interactive read-alouds can vary in format and focus, the following procedures provide only basic guidelines for implementation of this strategy:

1. Select the book to be used based on the chosen literacy focus. Also consider the age and maturity of the students in the class as well as their interests. Select books ranging from narratives to informational texts so that students are exposed to different text structures and language patterns, thereby expanding their knowledge and understanding of print.
2. After selecting a book for a read-aloud, read through it carefully before reading it to the students. Get a feel for the book's contents, its suspenseful moments, and the voice inflections and expressions to be used. Identify stopping points in the text where the literacy focus element can be highlighted. If the read-aloud requires more than one session, plan to stop at a suspenseful part so that students anticipate the next session. But be considerate, and do not leave students hanging for days at a time.
3. To begin a read-aloud session, invite students to sit quietly around you. If this is the first or only session for this book, take a minute to discuss the author and illustrator and give students a basic idea about the content of the book. This information is often provided on the back of the book or on the inside cover of the book jacket. In any subsequent sessions with the book, review with students what has happened thus far.
4. During the reading, adjust your voice tone and pace in accordance with what is happening in the book. Point out the literacy focus, drawing students into the text. In addition, help students make connections to the text.
5. Take time to show any pictures to all of the students and to answer any questions. Young students are more likely to ask spontaneous questions; nurture their inquisitiveness.
6. After reading, consider using extension activities to help students make connections and/or apply the literacy focus studied (see the boxed feature that follows).

Extending the Read-Aloud Experience

Take the time to discuss the book before reading it each day, but also leave time for discussion at the end of the read-aloud session. Go back and reread special sections, and talk about students' interpretations of particular events. Invite them to talk about why a character reacted in a certain way.
1. Provide opportunities for students to share their thoughts through journal entries in which they write about what was read, evaluate the material, ask questions about what is happening in the book, and make connections to themselves, to movies, and to other books.
2. For books that are long enough, let students work in groups to reenact select key events. Students enjoy reenacting stories. After reading Kevin Henkes's *Lilly's Purple Plastic Purse*, for example, students could retell the part of the story when her teacher takes away her purse and how Lilly reacts afterwards.
3. Have students embark on an Internet search for information about the author or illustrator. Many authors now have web pages that highlight their lives and books. The Children's Book Council features a web page with links to a variety of authors and illustrators. In addition, some authors (e.g., Jane Yolen) provide email addresses on their web sites so that their readers can correspond with them.

References

Barrentine, S. J. 1996. Engaging with reading through interactive read-alouds. *The Reading Teacher* 50: 36–43.

Cummins, C., and Stewart, M. 2006. Oral Language: A strong foundation for literacy instruction. In *Understanding and implementing Reading First initiatives: The Changing role of administrators*. 90–105. ed. C. Cummins. Newark, DE:IRA.

Henkes, K. 1996. *Lilly's purple plastic purse*. New York: Greenwillow Books.

Trelease, J. 1995. *The read-aloud handbook*. 4th ed. New York: Penguin Books.

SHARED READING

When to Teach		Group Size		Grade Level	
Before Reading	📖	One-on-One	👥	PreK–2	🏫
During Reading	📖	Small Group	👥	3–5	🏫
After Reading	📖	Whole Group	👥	6–8	🏫

R–Rationale

The shared reading experience helps students see reading as pleasurable and meaningful (Butler and Turbill 1987). It is a strategy that enables the teacher to model concepts about print by using a big book with large print while reading aloud to students. Shared reading can be one of the most effective ways to get students involved with print (Strickland and Morrow 1990). This strategy provides a risk-free environment for students to participate in real reading with guaranteed success, because students are free to join in the reading at their individual level of development. For example, students may join in only when they encounter a word that is part of their reading vocabulary.

E–Explanation

Shared reading generally uses big books—books large enough for a teacher to show to an entire group. These big books usually feature rhythm and rhyme; repetition of words, sentences, and elements of the story; and/or a basic storyline in relatively few words. Students can follow as the teacher reads, using a finger to track the words for students. Once they have discovered the book's patterns of rhyme, rhythm, and repetition, students can join in and may even be able to read the book alone during sustained silent reading. It is often useful to set aside time each day for reading and rereading favorite stories, rhymes, songs, poems, and chants. With each repetition of the book, students become more familiar with the content and are better able to join in as the teacher reads and to make predictions about what will happen next in the story. This method can be used with individuals, small groups, or large groups in the primary grades, which usually is considered prekindergarten through third grade.

A–Application

The teacher selects the book *Plenty of Penguins* by Sonia W. Black, which she knows her students will enjoy as they learn various facts about penguins. The teacher asks students to sit close enough to her and the book so that they can view the large print. The shared reading format presents the perfect opportunity to reinforce concepts about print with young students.

Before reading the teacher reviews the title and cover pictures and asks students to predict what they think the story will be about. The teacher also invites students to join in during the reading of the story whenever they wish.

During the reading the teacher uses her hand to track the print in order to reinforce the one-to-one correspondence between the spoken word and the written word. While reading key parts of the text, she pauses and lets the students fill in the missing text. For example, she reads these lines: "Penguins are big. And penguins are small." But she pauses before reading *small* and lets students use the preceding sentence to predict that the ending of the next sentence will be the opposite of *big*.

The teacher asks students to share which words sound alike, or rhyme, after she reads these lines:

What's black and white
and cute as can be?
A penguin.
That's me.
Do you want to meet
my family?

She says the word *be* and asks students to identify another word they hear that sounds a lot like the word *be*. To help them listen for these words, she rereads these lines and emphasizes the rhyming words *me* and *family*. As the students identify the words *me* and *family*, the teacher discusses what it is about the words that makes them sound alike. She also reinforces the left-to-right motion and the return sweep that we use when we move to the next line of the story. And she points out the end mark after the word *family*. She asks students what that end mark is called (i.e., question mark) and what it tells us when we read. *After reading* the teacher discusses with students what they learned from the story. The class decides to make a chart like the one shown here, which lists some of the facts they learned about penguins.

Facts about Penguins

What do penguins look like?	Where do penguins live?	What do penguins eat?
1. Penguins are black and white. 2. Some penguins have sharp, pointy feathers.	1. Penguins are found in South Africa, New Zealand, Australia, and Peru. 2. They live in great big groups—called colonies or rookeries.	1. They eat little fish. 2. Penguins eat squid. 3. They eat shrimp.

D–Delivery

Shared reading has a wide range of benefits, related especially to the fact that students are participating in the reading. This strategy also helps students develop concepts about reading and language—including concepts about story and narrative, rhythm and rhyme, the relationship between print and speech, and conventions such as punctuation—and it helps them with specific letter-sound correspondence and word recognition. The following are guidelines for a shared reading lesson:

1. Before doing the shared reading, select a text that will draw students into the reading, and practice reading it with intonation and phrasing.
2. Begin the shared reading by introducing the book. Discuss the author and illustrator, and give a brief overview of what the book is about. Consider highlighting relevant pages, such as the page with information about the author, the dedication page, and the title page. Always make sure that all students can easily see the book.
3. As you read the book, track the print with a pointer or your finger so that students can follow and certain concepts are reinforced, such as left-to-right and top-to-bottom directionality and one-to-one correspondence between the spoken word and the written word. Continue this practice in repeated readings.

4. Where appropriate, make and ask for predictions about the story (e.g., "I'll bet this is a story about . . . " or "I wonder what will happen next . . . "), explore key vocabulary, and invite students to repeat key words or phrases of the story, thereby joining in the reading.

5. After one or two readings, encourage the students to join in by repeating (or echoing) what has previously been read. For example, pause occasionally and let students fill in the anticipated language. On subsequent rereadings of the book, use sticky notes to cover words or word parts in order to focus on word structure (e.g., letter-sounds, onset-rime patterns, inflections, syllables) and language patterns (e.g., repetition, rhyme, unique words.)

6. After the shared reading, consider extension activities such as writing sentences from the story on chart paper but deleting one word and encouraging students to think of as many contextually plausible words as they can. For other extension options, refer to the boxed feature here.

Extending the Shared Reading

1. Write the story, or a portion of the story, on sentence strips so that students can retell or build the story using a pocket chart (McCracken and McCracken 1995).
2. Have the students write their own big book pages to extend the story, showing what would happen next.
3. Encourage the students to act out the story as a creative drama activity. Assign each student a character, and have the students wear index cards with their characters' names (Fisher and Medvic 2000).
4. Have the students dramatize the story with puppets as the characters (Fisher and Medvic 2000).

Note:
As previously mentioned, a typical shared reading in elementary classrooms generally involves reading of a big book and traditionally follows the described procedures. Shared reading for adolescent readers, however, can take a variety of forms depending on the purpose. The shared text might include excerpts from fiction and nonfiction, poetry, short stories, novels, or even texts used in literature circles. Students may have individual copies of the text or the teacher might show the text using some form of projection system. Reading the text then proceeds similarly to the delivery in a primary grade classroom with teacher reading demonstrations focusing on reading experiences, skills, and strategies more appropriate to this age group.

References

Black, S. 1999. *Plenty of penguins*. New York: Scholastic.

Butler, A., and J. Turbill. 1987. *Towards a reading-writing classroom*. Portsmouth, NH: Heinemann.

Fisher, B., and E. F. Medvic. 2000. *Perspectives on shared reading: Planning and practice*. Portsmouth, NH: Heinemann.

McCracken, M. J., and R. A. McCracken. 1995. *Reading, writing, and language*. 2nd ed. Winnipeg, Manitoba, Canada: Peguis.

Strickland, D. S., and L. M. Morrow. 1990. Sharing big books. *The Reading Teacher* 43: 342–43.

GUIDED READING

When to Teach		Group Size		Grade Level	
Before Reading	📖	One-on-One	👥	PreK–2	🏫
During Reading	📖	Small Group	👥	3–5	🏫
After Reading	📖	Whole Group	👥	6–8	🏫

R–Rationale

In the guided reading strategy, students read independently in small groups of four to six students as the teacher works with and monitors each student's use of reading strategies (Fountas and Pinnell 1996). The groups usually consist of students who are able to read at similar levels with support. A major goal of guided reading is to have students use reading strategies and their knowledge of story and text structure in order to successfully read the text. The ultimate goal is to have students read text independently and silently.

E–Explanation

Guided reading allows teachers to observe a small group of students as they develop an understanding of the reading process and practice their literacy skills. An important aspect of this strategy is that the reading groups are dynamic (Fountas and Pinnell 1996)—constantly changing according to the teacher's ongoing observation and assessment of each child. Thus, Rachel may be in a group with Susie and Timmy this week but, depending on her needs, may soon be switched to a different group.

The teacher has a different role in guided reading than in the other strategies we have looked at so far. With guided reading the teacher does not read a book to the students. Instead, the teacher monitors students' independent reading and uses a conversational approach, before and during the reading, to draw attention to vocabulary or syntactic structures that may be unfamiliar to the group.

While monitoring students, the teacher may choose to address one or two specific points a student is struggling with or to remind the student about a particular reading strategy that could be used (e.g., sound it out, reread, read ahead). The teacher also attempts to make the story meaningful, interesting, and personally relevant to students (Fountas and Pinnell 1996).

A–Application

The teacher selects a leveled text appropriate for a particular group of students. He then introduces the story to the students by doing a "picture walk" for each page of the book. As students make predictions about the text, the teacher "plants" vocabulary words they will encounter during the reading. For example, one of the Rigby books is about a zoo and each page features an animal along with two words—the article *a* and the animal's name. During the picture walk, the teacher talks to the students about what they see in each picture (e.g., lion) and what initial sound they hear in that word (e.g., /l/). Once the preview is complete, students read the text independently while the teacher monitors their use of reading strategies. As needed, the teacher steps in to assist students with a specific strategy by providing guidance and support. If students are all struggling with a particular strategy or literacy area, the teacher stops the reading and conducts a minilesson for all of them. As the students finish reading the book, the teacher has them immediately begin to reread it until all the students have read the story multiple times. After rereading, the students share their understanding of the story and discuss the strategies that they used while reading. This type of discussion reinforces students' metacognitive awareness.

D–Delivery

The difficult aspect of guided reading is that instruction, although preplanned to a point, has to be flexible and change according to students' needs while reading.

1. To begin the guided reading experience, select a book that is appropriate for a particular group and that will reinforce one or more particular skill areas. These skill areas can pertain to an area of word recognition, vocabulary, and/or comprehension. The children should be able to read the book with at least 90% accuracy.

2. Review the selected text carefully, and prepare an introduction that will draw students' attention to important words or structures and that will leave them with some questions to be answered through reading.

3. Before the students in the group read the story, preview it with them so that they engage in conversation about the story, ask questions, and notice information in the text. This is an important part of the guided reading experience; through previewing you can plant vocabulary and review reading strategies that students can use when they read the book independently. Begin the preview by reading the title and the author's and illustrator's names and then doing a picture walk through the story, page by page, while covering up the text. On each page, encourage students to examine the pictures: draw their attention to pictures that give clues about the text, and use the pictures to review some vocabulary they might need to read the book. For example, if one of the words students will encounter in the book is *cloud*, pause on a page with a picture of a cloud, and ask students what they see and then what sounds they hear at the beginning of *cloud* (/k/ and /l/). Also ask students what letters represent those sounds (*c* and *l*).

4. After the story has been introduced and previewed with the students, hand out a copy of the book to each group, and ask them to read the book (or a selected portion) softly aloud or silently. With younger readers, the reading should be softly aloud so that you can determine problem areas. You might ask young readers to point to the words as they read, to make sure they are actually reading the story and to help you assess their understanding of print convertion, etc.

5. As students read, move from student to student in order to observe and listen to each student's use of reading strategies as well as his or her fluency and comprehension. Help students who need assistance with a particular strategy or who ask for support with problem solving. For example, if a student is struggling with a particular word, you should step in and help the student work through a strategy to identify the word. If the word is a basic vocabulary word, the student might get assistance by looking at the picture again and/or breaking the word down by sounds or word parts.

6. Have students reread the story several times as you move from student to student. This type of repeated reading has been shown to benefit the comprehension of struggling readers. Perhaps ask students to reread with another student in the group. The buddy can help to reinforce whether the reading makes sense or can help with reading part of the text. If a student is struggling a great deal with a text, it may be that the text is too hard for that student. If so, adjust the student's book level for the next guided reading session, perhaps moving the student to another group that is reading a less difficult book.

7. After the students have read the story several times, have the group talk about the story together. Ask for personal responses to the story, return to the text for one or two teaching opportunities,

or evaluate students' understanding of what was read. Students can also participate in a word study that focuses on a phonic skill, sight word, or vocabulary word. For example, if the sight word *that* occurred in the book several times, students could use magnetic or foam letters to practice spelling the word.

8. Consider extension activities such as those found in the boxed feature.

Extending the Guided Reading Experience

1. Work with students to make a list of interesting words from the story, perhaps words of a certain part of speech (e.g., describing words, action words, naming words) or high-frequency words. Record these words on chart paper or word strips, and have students use magnetic or foam letters to build the words.
2. Look back through the book with students, and write targeted words on chart paper (e.g., words ending in *-ed*, *-s/-es*, or *-ing*; words beginning with certain sounds—sh, th, wh; different ways to say *said*, such as *shouted*, *whispered*).
3. Have the group write a big book using the pattern or language of guided-reading book as a model. Each student could be responsible for making one page of the big book. The pages could then be combined to make a class big book that could be placed in the class library for students to reread during independent reading.
4. Have students retell the story by acting it out with puppets or other props.
5. Have students draw a picture of and write about their favorite part of the story.

Note:
Adolescent students need guidance in their use of reading skills and strategies just as do primary grade students however a guided reading lesson will look differently. These students have most likely already learned how print works and how to use basic reading strategies but now need assistance in using more complex strategies in order to obtain deeper understandings. Guided reading at this level still requires focused teaching "at the point of need" to small groups of students, however, the procedure may be more in depth than the one previously described. General procedures might include: introducing the text, reading the text, discussing and revisiting the text, teaching for processing strategies, extending understanding, and word work.

Reference

Fountas, I. C., and G. S. Pinnell. 1996. *Guided reading: Good first teaching for all children.* Portsmouth, NH: Heinemann.

INDEPENDENT READING

When to Teach		Group Size		Grade Level	
Before Reading		One-on-One		PreK–2	
During Reading		Small Group		3–5	
After Reading		Whole Group		6–8	

R–Rationale

Independent reading is a method in which everyone—students and teacher—reads silently for a predetermined amount of time, using books and other reading materials they have chosen (Butler and Turbill 1987). "Free reading" is another name for this method, as are the acronyms SSR (sustained silent reading), USSR (uninterrupted sustained silent reading), DEAR (drop everything and read), and SQUIRT (sustained quiet reading time). Independent reading is indispensable because it gives students needed time to read and practice what they are learning and because it gives them the opportunity to independently read books in which they are interested. Such choice is an important motivator for students.

E–Explanation

There comes a time when our students need the time and opportunity to practice on their own what they have learned. They need opportunities where they are making choices about what they want to read, choices that will have a major impact on their motivation to read. Independent reading provides students with this opportunity. Key characteristics of a quality independent reading program include (Pilgreen 2000):

- Students are allowed to self-select the books and other materials that they will read during this time.
- The classroom library has numerous books and other reading material.
- The teacher provides encouragement and modeling and participates by also reading during the independent reading time.
- Students have a comfortable, pressure-free environment in which to read.
- Students select follow-up activities.
- Students are given an appropriate and sufficient amount of time in which to read.

A–Application

Before each session, the teacher makes sure that students have selected the books they will read and know where they will be reading. This teacher sometimes requires students to be in their seats and sometimes leaves the choice of seating up to them. Comfortable pillows and cushions work well for students who like to sit on the floor while reading.

During the independent reading session, the teacher models what is expected of students by selecting a book and finding a quiet place in the room to read. Independent reading is not a time for teachers to do daily attendance or grade papers; it is a time that everyone in the class reads a self-selected book for an extended period. If teachers do not participate in this process, it sends a message to students that this time is not valued. When possible, this teacher builds in a sharing session at the end of the independent reading time for students to discuss their thoughts and reflections about their books.

D–Delivery

There is no set procedure for implementation of independent reading, but a few guidelines will help to make it a successful part of your reading program.

1. Establish rules for the independent reading time, and go over these rules with students. Suggested rules include:
   - Everyone should be reading silently, including the teacher.
   - There should be no interruptions.
   - There should be no changing of books.
   - Students should have choice in selecting what they will read.
   - Students may bring books from home.
   - There should be a variety of types and formats of reading material to select.
2. Determine how long the sessions should last, based on what the students can easily manage. When starting out, keep sessions to no more than five to ten minutes, depending on the grade level. As students become accustomed to sustained silent reading, add additional minutes to the sessions. Use a timer to signal when the session is over.
3. Occasionally, provide students an opportunity to share their thoughts and reflections about their books.
4. Consider extension activities such as those shown in the boxed feature.

Extending the Independent Reading Experience

1. Have students read aloud from their books or share thoughts about their books while sitting in the "author's chair" (Harste, Short, and Burke 1988). The author's chair is a designated seat where students can sit when sharing their thoughts with other students about a particular book or piece of personal writing.
2. Have volunteers give sixty-second in-progress reviews of the highlights of their books. Let the class use these reviews to produce a newspaper section consisting of book recommendations. A final step might be a book and author luncheon (Pilgreen 2000).
3. Hold monthly "book sales" to allow students who have finished a book to "sell" it to others by explaining the main points of the book. Have students tell about the author, characters, and setting and give their personal reactions to the book (Revel-Wood 1988).

References

Butler, A., and J. Turbill. 1987. *Towards a reading-writing classroom.* Portsmouth, NH: Heinemann.

Harste, J. C., K. G. Short, and C. Burke. 1988. *Creating classrooms for authors.* Portsmouth, NH: Heinemann.

Pilgreen, J. 2000. *The SSR handbook: How to organize and manage a sustained silent reading program.* Portsmouth, NH: Heinemann.

Revel-Wood, M. 1988. Invitations to read, to write, to learn. In *Creating classrooms for authors: The reading-writing connection,* 169–179, ed. J. C. Harste, K. G. Short, and C. Burke. Portsmouth, NH: Heinemann.

LITERATURE CIRCLES

When to Teach		Group Size		Grade Level	
Before Reading	📖	One-on-One		PreK–2	🏫
During Reading	📖	Small Group	👥	3–5	🏫
After Reading	📖	Whole Group		6–8	🏫

R–Rationale

Literature circles are small, temporary discussion groups of students who have chosen to read the same story, poem, article, or book (Daniels 1994). This strategy provides students with opportunities to listen to others' perspectives and broaden their own perspectives about the text being read. It also provides time for students to work on skills and strategies targeted in short, focused minilessons (Atwell 1987; Calkins 1986).

E–Explanation

Literature circles are small groups of students sharing a common text. There are generally four to five groups with anywhere from four to six students in each group. This type of strategy is best used when students have developed enough proficiency to read relatively independently. It is possible to have literature circles with younger students in Grades K–2, but the teacher must provide more structure and guidance.

Since students select the group they wish to join based on their interest in a particular book, the groups are heterogeneous, with the students in a group sometimes at quite different levels. The groups meet once or twice a week to discuss their books, which students then read between the group meetings. Each literature circle lasts about two to three weeks or longer, depending on the book length and the number of pages or chapters each group decides to read between meeting sessions.

A–Application

The teacher prepares for literature circles by first deciding which books will be offered to students. She chooses these five books for her fifth-grade class:

- *Bridge to Terabithia* by Katherine Paterson
- *Dear Mr. Henshaw* by Beverly Cleary
- *Shiloh* by Phyllis Reynolds Naylor
- *The View from Saturday* by E. L. Konigsburg
- *There's a Boy in the Girls' Bathroom* by Louis Sachar

The teacher also plans to have four to five groups with four to six students in each group. Before the groups are formed, however, the teacher conducts a brief book talk about each book to familiarize students with the possible choices. Students then make their book selections based on their interests.

Cunningham and Allington (1994) recommend letting students choose from similar books or stories, since this can be a great motivator for reading. Once the groups have been formed, each group meets together to decide how much of the book its members will read before the first group conference session. Thereafter, the groups meet at least once a week. Between readings, each member of the group reads the designated number of pages and maintains a written response log with his or her thoughts about the book.

D–Delivery

Literature circles provide an opportunity for students to share their thoughts about a common text.

1. Before each new group of literature circles begins, select the books from which students may choose. The number depends mainly on the number of students in the classroom; usually, you should select about four to six books.
2. In addition to interests and reading levels, think in terms of potential for minilessons on specific skills or areas.
3. First introduce general routines and procedures to the class as a whole.
4. Then introduce the books to the class with a book talk about each choice. Try to capture the students' interest in the books, and give them enough information to guide their choices.
5. Have students meet with their groups (i.e., other students who selected the same book) and decide how many pages they will read before they meet for their first group conference session. Let students know how much overall time will be allowed for this set of literature circles. For example, the scenario might look like this:
   - Three weeks are planned for literature circles.
   - The groups meet two times a week.
   - The book has two hundred pages.

   Based on this information, the group members should read about seventy pages a week, or thirty-five pages between group sessions.
6. Have students keep a written response journal (also called a reading log or reading journal) in which they record their thoughts about and reactions to what they have read. This activity can be open-ended, with students having the freedom to write down whatever they choose, or it can be more structured, with students' responses following a given format.
7. When students meet for their designated group conference sessions, have them bring their books and response logs. Let them take turns sharing what they think about the book. They can also ask questions of each other about parts of the book that did not make sense, that they liked a lot, that they disagreed with, and so on. Initially, students tend to simply retell the story, but with guidance from you and other students, they will begin to discuss other aspects of the book, make personal connections, and even compare the book with other books they have read.
8. At the end of the time for literature circles, consider asking students to do an extension activity. Because extension projects can sometimes be time-consuming and take time away from the reading, writing, talking, and reflecting that is the focus of literature circles, suggest that students do one project every six to nine weeks instead of with every book. Project ideas are included in the boxed feature.

Extending the Literature Circles

Students can work alone or with their groups on any of these projects that relate to their books.
1. Highlight specific parts of the book by producing a comic strip, accordion book, or story map.
2. Create a book cover or character book mark.
3. Make a scrapbook, story quilt, or alphabet book.
4. Engage in a panel debate.
5. Write a script and rehearse for a readers' theater performance.
6. Write a newspaper article that summarizes the story.

References

Atwell, N. 1987. *In the middle: Writing, reading, and learning with adolescents*. Portsmouth, NH: Heinemann.

Calkins, L. M. 1986. *The art of teaching writing*. Portsmouth, NH: Heinemann.

Cunningham, P. M., and R. L. Allington. 1994. *Classrooms that work: They can all read and write*. New York: Harper-Collins.

Daniels, H. 1994. *Literature circles: Voice and choice in the student-centered classroom*. York, ME: Stenhouse.

Index

Information 3, 5–6, 9–10, 13, 35, 53, 82–84, 95, 99–101, 107–108, 111, 114, 117, 120, 125, 127–128, 131–135, 138–139, 143, 146–147, 149, 151, 154–157, 159, 168–169, 172, 175, 180
Instruction 1–3, 9, 11, 20, 35–37, 41–42, 48, 50, 61, 65, 70, 73, 77, 79, 80, 84, 87, 104, 111, 147–149, 152, 167–168, 175
Intonation 65–70, 74, 172

Knowledge 1, 5, 8, 30, 35, 39, 42–44, 47–48, 50, 55, 79–80, 91–92, 94, 98, 101, 104–105, 107, 111, 113–114, 119, 122–124, 127–128, 132–133, 138, 145–147, 156, 159, 161, 168, 179, 174

Language 1–3, 5, 7–9, 11, 13, 16, 19, 20–21, 25–26, 35, 46, 79, 94, 145–146, 167–169, 172–173, 176
Listening 1, 5, 17, 23–25, 27, 46, 55, 76, 121, 168
Literacy 1–2, 61, 65, 147, 167–169, 174–175
Literacy development 79, 168
Literature Circles 155, 179–180

Manipulate 19–20, 27, 53
Meaning 9, 13, 43, 46, 48–49, 65, 74, 79–80, 84–85, 89–90, 92, 94–95, 98, 101, 104, 109, 111, 127, 134, 136–138, 147, 149, 154
Metacognition 111
Metacognitive readers 111
Model 4, 13–14, 16, 21, 24, 48, 53, 55, 65–70, 73, 83, 87–88, 90, 110, 111, 122, 131, 133–138, 143, 155, 161, 164, 168, 171, 176–178
Monitor 5, 17, 111, 119, 136, 147, 174

Open sorts 109–110
Oral language 1–18, 26, 145, 167–168
Orthography 35

Patterns and relationships 91–92, 109–110
Phonemes 19–20, 23–24, 27, 35
Phonemic awareness 19–34, 35, 53, 61, 65, 152, 167
Phonics 19–20, 23, 35–64, 65, 152, 167
Phonogram 19–20, 41, 55, 58
Phonology 35
Picture Walk 123, 174–175
Prediction 5–6, 17–18, 94, 96–98, 113, 119–120, 123–124, 126, 156, 168–169, 171, 173–174
Prior knowledge 5, 42, 92, 94, 111, 113, 127, 156
Process 1, 10–12, 17, 21–22, 27, 39–40, 44, 46–47, 49, 53–54, 60, 62, 65–66, 69–70, 85, 87, 90, 94, 101, 111, 119–123, 133–138, 143, 147–149, 152, 155–156, 160, 163–165, 174, 176, 178
Productive talk 7
Prosody 65, 70, 72

Questioning 131, 134–137, 142

Read-alouds 49, 65, 76–77, 79, 98, 153, 167–169
Reading processes 65, 111, 174
Repeated readings 65–67, 69, 70, 75–77, 172, 175
Retelling 1, 13–14, 125, 143, 165, 169, 173, 176, 180
Risk-free environment 171

Scaffold 13–14, 61, 136
Schema 113, 124
Segment 5–6, 19–20, 23–24, 31, 46, 48–49, 66, 68–70, 112, 120, 134–136, 138–139, 153
Segmentation 19
Shared Reading 41–42, 49, 77, 79, 171–173
Skill 2–3, 7, 13, 17, 19–21, 23, 25, 31, 36, 65, 68, 75, 91, 104, 111, 113–114, 117, 121, 136, 145, 148, 152, 167, 169, 173–174, 176, 179–180
Sorting 31, 33–34, 53, 54–55, 58, 92, 109–110
Sound-symbol relations 36
Sound-symbol relationships 44
Spelling 20, 35, 43–44, 46, 53–55, 62, 152, 155, 176
Story elements 96, 142, 145–146, 168
Storytelling 1
Student engagement 134, 148
Strategy 1, 3, 7, 13–17, 23, 31, 35, 41, 46, 48, 50, 53, 56–57, 60, 62, 65, 68, 72–73, 76, 79–81, 87–89, 91–92, 94, 96, 98, 100–101, 104, 109, 111, 113, 115, 117, 119, 121–122, 127, 129, 131–138, 140, 142–143, 145, 148–149, 152, 154, 156, 158–162, 164–165, 167–169, 17–177, 179
Summarize 10, 13, 18, 136–137, 145, 180
Summary 17–18, 115–116, 130, 138–140, 145, 154
Systematic 35–36, 41, 43, 70

Talk 1, 3, 5–12, 15, 17–18, 24, 27, 42, 49, 58–61, 68, 74, 76, 85, 87, 89, 100, 109–110, 115–116, 118–119, 122, 137–139, 141, 154, 161, 164, 169, 174–175, 179–180
Think-alouds 88, 131
Thinking 1, 5, 8, 13, 17–19, 91, 110, 113–114, 117–119, 121–124, 132–133, 147, 156, 162, 163–164

Visual interpretation 129
Vocabulary 7–8, 12, 25, 31, 35, 43, 48, 65, 77, 79–110, 123–124, 126, 145, 149, 154, 167–168, 173–176

Word family 43–44, 50, 58, 59–60, 172
Word recognition 48, 65, 172, 175
Word study 46, 61, 63, 176
Writing 10–11, 20, 35, 50, 61, 115, 117, 121, 140, 145, 147–166, 167–168, 173, 178, 180
Writing process 147–149, 152, 164
Writing prompts 162
Written response 154, 180